Prospero's Magic

Magic

active Learning strategies for the teaching of Literature

MICHAEL DEGEN

TELEMACHOS PUBLISHING

Second Edition
Telemachos Publishing
PO Box 460387
Garland, TX 75046-0387
972-205-9964

Library of Congress Catalog Card Number: 00-104889
ISBN: 0966512545
Printed in the United States of America

www.telemachospublishing.com

But this rough magic
I here abjure; and when I have required
Some heavenly music (which even now I do)
To work mine end upon their senses, that
This airy charm is for, I'll break my staff,
Bury it certain fathoms in the earth,
And deeper than did ever plummet sound
I'll drown my book.

The Tempest 5:i:50-57

Read this first, please ─────────────────

Dear Educator,

The activities in this text are designed to get students involved with and excited about what they are reading. You may, if you wish, use any activity as it exists within this text, or you may decide to adapt it to meet your specific needs. Any page within this text may be reproduced for instructional use only.

One of the foundation beliefs behind my teaching is that educators need to relinquish control—gradually and in an organized fashion—over the school year. We need, in other words, to teach our students how to read and discuss and involve themselves in a work of literature without being totally dependent upon the instructor. This does not happen by magic. It does not happen when we merely "assign" reading without preparing students for entry into the imaginary world and without showing them how to talk about what they have read, and it will not happen if we "assign" reading and expect students to sit still for our words of wisdom about it. I find that it happens slowly, methodically, over time as they become more and more accustomed to being intimately connected to the process of making meaning out of what they read. One of the goals of this book is to help teachers who are looking for ways to activate that connection between the reader and the world the author has created. The magic, then, occurs not with what the teacher does but with what they—the students, the readers—do with the literature.

The first two chapters focus on thinking skills and discussion approaches that can be employed with any work of literature. Although Great Expectations and The Count of Monte Cristo, for example, are the specific texts used in the first two discussion strategies of the second chapter, the methodologies will work with any literary text.

The same holds true for the specific works of literature mentioned in the activities of chapters three, four, and five. Rather than explain each activity in general terms, I provide a detailed description of it when used with a particular work of literature. This is not meant to suggest in any way that only these literary works can be connected with these activities, nor is there any suggestion that the activities as described cannot be amended or changed in any way. Of course, they can—and should—be changed to suit your needs and the needs of your students.

I finish this text with an appendix of ideas, especially for new teachers, concerning classroom management. With rare exceptions, creating the kind of classroom that allows for creative and fruitful activity takes a sense of organization that many of us need years in mastering.

Sincerely,

Michael Degen
www.jesuitcp.org
gargery@yahoo.com

table of contents

IT'S THE TEACHER, NOT THE COMPUTER

School boards are locating monies to make each student's classroom the beneficiary of the latest in high-tech educational developments, for no school district wants to be left behind in the Information Age's computer revolution. As we move further into a new century, a prevailing idea seems to be that we hook up each classroom to the Internet and watch American secondary education, the laggard of the first world, catapult forward.

What will catapult forward is, however, an increase in intellectual lethargy, says author-astronomer Dr. Clifford Stoll, himself one of the pioneers of the Internet. Computers, no matter how visually thrilling, merely deliver facts, merely operate on the lowest level of Bloom's taxonomy. Stoll states that "on the surface, all of these wonderful teaching machines are teaching reading, writing, arithmetic, physics, science, history, but the reality is they're teaching facts, but not skills."

Moreover, multimedia in the classroom, like filmstrips of days old, provide an excuse to avoid thinking, he insists. The more time online, the more time essential skills—reading, writing, thinking—abate. The promise of this new technology—information and power—is false. Stoll recalls a striking allusion to this age: "It's the same thing that the devil promised Faust! Omniscience and omnipotence."

The teacher, Stoll insists, provides the opportunity to learn, to develop genuine academic skills. In fact, this computer scientist believes that the most valuable lessons he learned were not at the computer but in his English classroom:

> My high school English teacher forced us to read Shakespeare. Forced us to write an essay every Thursday. Forced us to argue and stand up in class and state exactly what we'd read. We didn't like it; we'd much rather have just played Nintendo.... I'd rather play with the computer. If you want to be able to write, if you want to be able to speak out in public, if you want to be able to cogently put arguments together, you don't do it by fooling around on computers. You do it through taking tough classes. By having committed, inspired teachers. (2F)

Stoll's English teacher forced upon his classes critical thinking activities, strategies that engaged students' intellects. Today, even more important than in Stoll's high school years, teachers can counter the current wave of technological hysteria by using active learning strategies that require students to argue persuasively, to read critically, to write cogently.

English teachers, especially, are charged with engaging students with the intellectual creations of the master writers. It is not through anything a computer provides that students will learn to love reading literature; it is the teacher who must provide the environment in the classroom that allows students to work with—indeed, to wrestle with—the author's words and enter the created world of that writer.

All the activities in Prospero's Magic are designed to generate student involvement, both intellectual and physical, and will entice a larger percentage of students to participate in the learning process through the following objectives:

- to practice oral communication skills;
- to develop critical thinking skills: drawing conclusions, using deductive and inductive reasoning, organizing ideas, creating focused thesis statements;
- to help students connect their lives to the material;
- to develop patterns of independent and enthusiastic learning;
- to accommodate a variety of learning styles;
- to allow students to express individual creativity;
- to practice large group communication skills;
- to provide alternative assessments;
- to provide clear directions and expectations for student performance;
- to challenge students toward the magis, a Latin term that means "the thirst for more," the desire to go beyond mediocrity.

The primary focus of these teaching strategies is that they bring to the fore—and help to carry out—the crucial task of the teacher of great books: how to enable students to talk constructively about the literature. In her article "Writing as a Mode of Learning," Janet Emig explains the distinctions between listening, reading, writing, and talking. What is significant to the current discussion is Emig's explanation of the difference between listening (students listening to a lecture, for example) and talking (as when students make an oral presentation). She writes that "listening is creating or

re-creating but not originating a verbal construct.... Talking is creating and originating a verbal construct."

Shaping our teaching philosophy around active learning provides several benefits. In Inspiring Active Learning: A Handbook for Teachers, Merrill Harmin explains that these strategies help reach all types of children, especially those more reticent and even withdrawn. In addition, she believes that active learning strategies promote the following benefits: the dignity of students, by helping them experience genuine academic success; intellectual energy, as students become engaged rather than passively receiving information from lectures or multimedia presentations; self-management, since students learn how to make responsible choices and to use time management skills; community, where students feel more comfortable sharing information and working with other students; awareness, as students become more respectful of other's comments by attentively listening and responding to the ideas discussed.

Please note, too, that all these activities are adaptable to a particular situation. Change time frames, aspects of directions, number of players, for example. Some of the activities can be copied and used as is (evaluation rubrics, game directions, discussion directions), while others are models (Romeo & Juliet Readers' Theatre, Odyssey Book Project) that may be adapted to the material the class is currently studying.

Emig, Janet. "Writing as a Mode of Learning." College Composition and Communication 28 (May 1977):122-28. Rpt. in The St. Martin's Guide to Teaching Writing. Eds. Robert Connors and Cheryl Glenn.

Harmin, Merrill. Inspiring Active Learning: A Handbook for Teachers. Virginia: ASCD, 1994.

Stoll, Clifford. "Internet Pioneer Reverses Course, Calling Computers Mostly a Waste." Dallas Morning News. 4 August 1998: F2.

one

Critical Thinking Games for Developing Perspicacious Readers

LEARNING HOW TO READ PERCEPTIVELY

What kind of readers do we as English teachers want our students to become? What do we want them to be aware of as they read? How do we teach them to focus on certain key elements in a story line or poem? These are questions that beginning teachers always need to ask themselves before they start working with students, and those of us who have been teaching for a while must on occasion reassess what we know, what our goals ought to be, and what approaches we wish to use in order to reach them.

Reading literature is no easy task. Students must be taught how to read literature. It is not a skill with which one is born, nor is it a skill that students have mastered by the time we see them on the secondary level. It is a skill we as teachers are still mastering for ourselves, and we want our students to begin to apply certain principles that will make them not only lifelong readers but readers who do so with a keen eye. In view of that, I begin teaching reading each year with a fairly simple text, but one that contains all of the elements that a perceptive reader knows.

CHECKLIST FOR PERSPICACIOUS READING

At the beginning of the year, before I begin a novel or other major literary work, I provide each student with a copy of guidelines—a checklist, if you will—for reading intelligently. You will find this checklist on the following page. To practice these skills, I sometimes use contemporary song lyrics. I especially like U2's "I Still Haven't Found What I'm Looking For" as this song contains all of the elements on the guidelines for reading. We then apply these reading strategies to a larger work of literature. An understanding of the categories in this checklist not only enriches their reading but also provides a way for students to elaborate their discussions during the games that will be featured in this chapter of Prospero's Magic.

A CHECKLIST FOR PERSPICACIOUS READING

For purposes of appreciating the world created by the writer—to understand perhaps on a deeper level specific literary elements such as character, situation, setting, conflict, theme, motif, and tone—the perceptive reader notices the following in a literary text:

DIDLS = ___ **d**iction ___ **i**magery ___ **d**etails ___ **l**anguage ___**s**yntax

___ **d**iction: The author's choice of particular words. Since so many ideas have a variety of words that writers can employ in order to achieve their intended effect, the careful reader considers why certain word choices have been made rather than others.

___ **i**magery: The image—or picture—that is made concrete in the reader's mind because of the words (diction and language) the author uses. Imagery can be both literal (how the words physically describe the object, character, or event) and/or figurative (where abstract ideas are expressed vividly through the use of literary devices such as the metaphor, personification, allusion, and the symbol).

___ **d**etails: Specific facts concerning a character, situation, object, etc.. Sometimes, the details a writer omits have a certain importance that ought not be overlooked.

___ **l**anguage: Language broadly refers to the level or type of diction used by the writer—the degree of formality or informality in the words, whether the writer uses colloquial speech, slang, or jargon.

___ **s**yntax: The structure of words in a group—how the author grammatically arranges words within a sentence.

ARCHETYPES

___ Character types, images, and/or patterns within stories that are said to be universal (found within all cultures). Common character archetypes include the hero, the wise old man or woman, the temptress, the savior, the trickster, the mentor, the rebel, and the servant; pattern archetypes include the journey and the initiation; nature archetypes include the sea, the garden, the rose, the whale, the vulture, and the snake.

ALLUSIONS

___Often a literary text will make a reference, explicit or implicit, to something— an event, a character, an idea—from literature, art, history, mythology, the Bible, or other major religious texts.

REPETITION

___ The reader should take notice of any key words, images, archetypes, or other details that are repeated more than once.

CRITICAL THINKING GAMES

quotation game

lyric game

tournament of scholars

question-answer game

PRESENTATION

I begin these games at a variety of stages during the reading of a novel, story, play, or poetry. For example, I usually play the Tournament of Scholars after we're past the halfway point of a novel. The Quotation Game and the Question-Answer Game work at any point in the study of the literature. The Lyric Game is used to practice "raw" responses, drawing conclusions about poems that have not yet been discussed by the entire class or the teacher; this provides students an opportunity to start discussion themselves, proving, too, that they can indeed understand poetry, that they can find logical meaning as they work with each other on the poem.

OBJECTIVES

• Students will practice orally those skills of literary argument that they will also employ in the writing of essays: clear thesis and topic sentences, logical organization, coherence, supporting evidence;
• Students will work the text itself, exploring diction, imagery, details, language, syntax, archetypes, allusions, and repetitions—and they will explain how these elements connect with developing themes;
• Students will practice group communication skills: presentation, organization, compromise, etc..

SCORING

Follow a general rubric for scoring, one that reinforces the writing skills emphasized in class during the year and demonstrates the interconnectedness of reading and writing skills.

GENERAL GAME SCORING GUIDELINES*

Evaluation elements	
Clear topic sentence/thesis statement	1 point
Logical textual support	1 point
Elaboration of textual support	1 point
Transitional sentences and other transitional devices	1 point
Obvious method of organization: time, place, space	1 point

* based on the writing rubric used throughout the school year in Crafting Expository Argument: Practical Approaches to the Writing Process for Students & Teachers.

TIPS FOR IMPLEMENTATION

1. While teams present, take notes on points you wish to address with the class after the round.
2. Never tell the teams the score until the tournament is over!
3. After you finish a round, take time to share your notes with the class. This provides a great opportunity to praise and to correct illogical interpretations, to reread parts of the text all groups missed, to extend the elaboration of a good idea.
4. When organizing teams, place an "A" student, a "B" student, and a "C" student in the group.
5. You can also use this game for graded discussion. Make a chart with all the students' names, and keep a record of the types of responses they give. See, for example, the "discussion quiz grading form," p. 33.
6. Encourage students to make connections with other works of literature.
7. Encourage students to use the literary terms you have reinforced in class.

BENEFITS OF THE GAMES

1. Provides an opportunity to practice universal writing skills and speaking skills.
2. Addresses statewide speaking objectives.
3. Provides an efficient way to practice the AP writing prompts.
4. Employs active learning strategies and draws on the benefits of group work.
5. Demonstrates to students that they do have the ability to develop intellectual ideas independent of the teacher.
6. Provides a practical activity for closure to a unit.
7. Can be adapted to use with any genre: novel, short story, play.
8. Playing the games provides a break in instructional routine—especially for longer works of literature.

game 1

quotation game

FORMAT

Teacher types several excerpts or single-line quotations from a novel, short story, play, or poem. These are separated on strips of paper.

DIRECTIONS

1. Each team chooses a quotation.
2. Team members have up to four minutes to prepare their discussion of the quotation.
3. After preparation, the first presenting team takes command. All members of the team must speak, or each member must make a substantial comment at least once during the class period. Teams will be penalized for not meeting this requirement. All other teams must listen carefully during the presentation. While presenting, team members have up to two minutes to cover, as completely as possible, the following areas:

   A. Plot Details: Who is the speaker? What is occurring at this point?   1 pt.
   B. Interpretation: What is significant about this passage? Does it reveal something about character? theme? conflict? Elaborate.   1-3 pts.
   C. Analysis: What tools does the author use to communicate your answer to "B"? diction? details? imagery? dialogue? allusion?   1-3 pts.

4. After the team presents, the remaining teams have an opportunity to make extemporaneous comments about the passage. Each listening team may now have up to one minute to add any additional comments that have not been mentioned. However, teams will lose points if they merely repeat comments stated by the previous team.
5. After each listening team has had an opportunity to respond extemporaneously, the next presenting team begins with its quotation.
6. When all presenting teams have had their turns and the extemporaneous comments have taken place, one round is over. You may have as many rounds as you wish of this game.

PRIZE

Plan your own system of rewards. I issue quiz passes to the members of the winning team and another quiz pass to the one student with the most creative responses.

game **2**

question-answer game

FORMAT

1. Each student is assigned membership to a group that consists of three to four people. The teacher has a list of students in each group, a list used to mark points for each individual. These points go towards a team total.
2. A student moderator is chosen to call on students who will ask and answer questions about the piece of literature the class is currently studying.
3. The teacher will determine how many days the game will last. Depending on the work of literature, this game has lasted anywhere from a full class period to all or parts of five consecutive class periods.

DIRECTIONS

1. Students must raise their hands when asking or answering a question.
2. When a student asks or answers a question, his or her team will receive points determined by the overall quality of question or answer.
3. The team that has accumulated the most points either at the end of the day or unit will receive a quiz pass.
4. The following point system is used to rate each question or answer.

QUESTIONS
1 pt. = knowledge level question: e.g. what happened, etc.
2 pts. = question involving analysis of text. e.g. on page #___, why do you think it's significant that Gatsby says, "..."?
3 pts. = a superior, perceptive question

ANSWERS
1 pt. = knowledge level
2 pts. = involves some analysis
3 pts. = involves critical analysis, discussion of diction, application of theme, contemporary connections.

DEDUCTIONS
2 pts. = derision of opponents
2 pts. = repeating analysis already mentioned

BONUS POINTS
5 pts. = every member of team has engaged in active questions-answers.

game 3

lyric game

FORMAT

The teacher prepares a list of poems. The teacher either selects the same poem for all groups of three to four students to explicate orally or uses a lottery system. The teacher informs group members how much time they have to prepare their commentary. (I give anywhere from 15 to 30 minutes.) At the end of this time, groups must stop. Each group then has a prescribed number of minutes to present its explication. (I usually allow up to six minutes.) The teacher scores each response according to these traits: clarity of thesis, organization, textual support, originality, participation of all group members. After all groups have finished, begin a second round with a new poem.

DIRECTIONS

1. Each team will have ___ minutes for preparation and ___ minutes to present its case.
2. Each person in the group must speak during the presentation.
3. Repetition of exact ideas will not receive credit.
4. Once the round begins, teams may not talk amongst themselves.

Please use this language when presenting; students should say,

> √ "The poem_____ is attempting to say/assert/argue that _____ (thesis)"
> For example: "The poem 'Sonnet 29' asserts that humans are capable of moving beyond despondency through the use of memory."
> √ "First, (first aspect of the aforementioned thesis statement) is supported by..."
> For example: "First, the initial two quatrains establish with imagery the narrator's depressed condition. For instance,...."
> √ "Second, (second aspect of the thesis statement) is supported by... (diction, for example)
> For example: "In the third quatrain, the narrator begins to indicate the use of his memory. For instance, in line...."

PRIZE

Plan your own system of rewards. I issue quiz passes to the members of the winning team and another quiz pass to the one student with the most creative responses.

game 4

tournament of scholars

FORMAT

Each group of three students prepares at least three open-ended questions (see next page for types of questions that might be created), or each member may be assigned to write two questions, from which the best three questions can be designated for the tournament and the remainder can be employed as alternatives in case one of the designated questions is employed beforehand by another team. Questions cover details in the literary work that have been assigned as reading. In addition, each question must be accompanied by a written answer that cites text. A specific amount of class time may be set aside for the preparation of these questions.

DIRECTIONS

1. Two triads at a time will face off. Team A will read one of its questions. That question will be awarded one, two, or three points, depending on quality, originality, depth, etc.. See suggested rubric at the top of p. 20.

2. Team B has a total of eight minutes to respond. This time may be divided between preparation and response, however the team chooses. Some teams, for example, spend four minutes preparing and four minutes giving their oral answer. This response will be awarded one, two, or three points, depending on the completeness of their answer, their knowledge and citation of textual evidence, and their understanding of larger thematic patterns in the work.

3. After their response, the members of Team A will have an opportunity to provide a one minute extension. This is an opportunity for the team to make comments heretofore unaddressed. Here the team members may use their own previously written response, as well as any other ideas they might have developed; this extension is awarded points.

4. After this extension or rebuttal, the teams outside the pair-off may each have one minute to add information that neither team addressed. The teacher awards the outside ring of teams points, using the rubric. [Note: The teacher will vary the order in which teams answer. For example, if John's team responds immediately after the extension, the next round his team might answer last.]

5. Once the outside teams have contributed, Team B now presents its question to Team A. After their pair-off, Teams C and D begin.

TYPES OF QUESTIONS TO CONSIDER WHEN READING

CHARACTER QUESTIONS
Questions that inquire into the motivations or characteristics of individual characters in the novel can be very helpful as will any questions that require us to draw conclusions or make inferences about a character because of what he or she says or does. Again, do not ask general or broad questions, such as What are the themes of the book?

QUESTIONS CONCERNING THE AUTHOR'S PURPOSE OR TECHNIQUE
These questions will seek to figure out why the author seems to emphasize a specific trait or habit of a character, why the author repeats a certain idea, why the author uses a specific simile or metaphor, why the author creates an image or a symbol at a specific point in the story.

QUESTIONS THAT REQUIRE MAKING PERCEPTIVE CONNECTIONS WITHIN THE TEXT
These questions will concentrate on how one part of the story is connected to another, how one character is like another, or how one sequence of events is like another.

QUESTIONS THAT REQUIRE MAKING PERCEPTIVE CONNECTIONS AMONG STORIES
These questions will demonstrate your ability to perceive how characters, situations, themes, etc., in one story compare and/or contrast with characters, situations, and themes from other stories.

QUESTIONS ABOUT THE NARRATOR AS NARRATOR
Is this a first person narration? third person omniscient? How does this perspective influence the story?

QUESTIONS THAT APPLY THE NOVEL TO LIFE IN GENERAL
Throughout the novel you may find situations that apply to people or events today. Again, general questions will not be appropriate. Your question should refer to a specific situation in the story.

QUESTIONS FROM CRITICAL RESEARCH
You may read a short comment or passage from a critical essay and ask a group to react—agree or disagree, providing textual evidence for the position. Always cite source and author.

OTHER SUGGESTIONS
1. Designate each team with a letter or number or creative nickname beforehand. Once all teams have paired off, the first round is over. In the second round, be sure different teams pair off.
2. An even number of teams works very well. However, if you have an odd number of teams, rotate the pair-offs; in other words, let A ask B, B ask C, C ask A, etc....

AWARDS
Develop your own system of rewards. I use the quiz pass for the top two teams.

Points for questions

1 pt. = general question about a theme already discussed in class; question that might be too general or broad; a question that lacks precise focus and may need clarification by the teacher.

2 pts. = a well-written question that requires careful analysis of text; a question that seeks a different angle to previously discussed ideas in class.

3 pts. = outstanding and original idea; a question that introduces something new to our discussion of the literature; a question that points the class to a pattern, image, metaphor, or some other fascinating repetition in the text previously overlooked; this question may inquire about connections to other works of literature.

Points for answers

1 pt. = answer lacks textual reference; answer is general; argument not organized; main points a bit confusing.

2 pts. = answer includes textual reference; more analysis of diction, imagery, details needed; organization present.

3 pts. = thorough answer; creative response; extensive use of text; argument organized well; main points identified clearly.

Additional Option

The Final Round of the Tournament of Scholars

Use after each team has completed two rounds.

Format

This speed round will consist of several questions generated by the teams—the alternative or extra questions not used in the two rounds of the tournament thus far. They may also be questions generated by the teacher. If you wish, these questions may be given to students ahead of time, preferably over a weekend, or the final round may begin immediately following the completion of the first two rounds.

DIRECTIONS

The teacher recites a question. After an all-team one minute prep, each team will have one minute to respond to the question chosen by the teacher. After the general one minute prep, no talking or additional preparation is allowed. With each new question, the teacher will randomly select the order in which teams respond. This will then prevent one team from always speaking first. No points will be awarded for repetition of responses.

TOURNAMENT SCORE CARD

Group members	Rd. 1 Q 1	Ext.	Ans.	Rd. 2 Q 2	Ext.	Ans.	Outside Pts.	Final Rd.	Total Pts.

two

Opening Students' Mouths—and Minds

Talking about literature teaches skills, provides alternative assessment

WHY DISCUSS DEEPLY

The most important part of the experience of reading a great book may very well be talking about it with others who have also read it. By discussing a literary work, the author's world comes alive for a perceptive reader. Thorough discussion allows people to think deeply about the text they're reading and to keep thinking about all of it—from the first chapter until we reach the end.

I sometimes feel that we as teachers have too often followed a pattern: We've assigned material to be read, lectured upon it, perhaps—if we have time—discussed it a bit with students, and tested them over the literature. Then we move on to something else. I wonder how much of the novel or epic or play stays with a reader when the experience has been so perfunctory and the discussion of the rich world of the story so minute in comparison to what could be discussed. When we as literature teachers feel the need—or pressure—to cover x amount of material in a school year, we too often end up providing a superficial gloss of the author's created world and miss the opportunity to teach our students how to discover the depth and beauty of that world, an opportunity for discovery that

meaningful discussion provides.

DISCUSSION FORMATS

At present, I use two discussion formats: the lengthy ongoing discussion test—covering the entire time we'll be working with a specific literary work—and the shorter discussion quiz—covering a series of poems or a few chapters or scenes within a larger work and lasting for up to two class periods. All discussion is graded, a matter I discuss in greater detail on p. 29 in "Why Grading Matters—and Cliffs Notes, too."

One purpose of using discussion as a means of assessment is to enhance in the eyes of all the students the importance of speaking up in class, of sharing their ideas. That's why I keep track of who speaks up and, with the help of a different student moderator each day, will keep an eye out for students who raise their hands and have not spoken up much heretofore. In addition, I want students to understand that what they have to say has value, much more value than what I have to say about the story. That's why I do very little lecture—in fact, almost none or none, depending on the text. The last thing I want is for students to parrot me when they begin writing their essays at the end of a novel or play.

Getting Students Started

From small group to large group—the ongoing discussion test

Discussing The Count of Monte Cristo

Teaching students how to discuss a work of literature so that the discussion creates meaning is a step-by-step process. A discussion ought not become merely a platform for the verbose—including teachers—or a chaotic jumble flitting from one topic to another. Ideally, the entire English department would have an organized approach to teaching discussion skills that eventually find students in charge of the entire discussion. Certain variations of the inner-outer circle approach to discussion seek to accomplish this. What follows, however, is a format by which all students in the class are involved in the process, one that begins in small group situations and leads toward full-class discussion of the text. Students are first divided into small groups on specific topics stemming from the literary work—in this case, Alexandre Dumas' The Count of Monte Cristo (the Bantam Classic edition); they discuss their responses together thoroughly and then present their responses to the class, each member of the group being required to handle a fair share of the presentation. While the small group presents, the remaining students take brief notes. After the small group presentation, the rest of the class joins the discussion, elaborating points already made, agreeing and/or disagreeing with the presenters. The small group, thus, jumpstarts the large group discussion.

KEEPING STUDENTS ON THE SAME PAGE

Provide a syllabus ahead of time for students and for parents. Use a mix of tests and daily quizzes to ensure students do not put off reading, and so you'll know who is reading and how well. Phone parents when needed.

A sample testing schedule
Mon., Nov. 16: Chpts. 1-16
Mon., Nov. 23: Chpts. 17-31
Tues., Dec. 1: Chpts. 32-51
Tues., Dec. 8: Chpts. 52-73

Daily quizzes
Break down the weekly readings into daily segments: Day 1, Chpts. 1-3; Day 2, Chpts. 4-7; etc.. Ask one or two questions per day. I ask questions requiring very short answers and allow a matter of five to ten seconds to complete. Students quickly exchange papers, grade, and turn them in. Next class day, the quiz papers are returned and used for that day's quiz.

GRADING RUBRIC FOR DISCUSSION

The discussion is an ongoing test that is completed when the novel is finished. Points are allotted based on the type of student participation both in the large group discussion and the small group presentation that precedes it.

- Questions of **clarification.** 1 pt.
- Responses **based on details** from text. 1 pt.
- Responses based on details from the text that **elaborate upon a named classmate's previous comment,** such response being more than a mere repetition. 2 pts.
- Responses that **take the class into the text** and require the class to read certain passages, **the significance of which is then explained** by the respondent. 3 pts.
- Responses of overarching quality: These responses **make connections** between events, themes, and/or characters in this and some other literary work, or **apply** events, themes, and characters from the story to our lives today, or **establish significant ties** between actions in one part of the text with actions in another part. 4 pts.

FOUNDATION QUESTIONS FOR MONTE CRISTO DISCUSSIONS

For many young readers, a novel like The Count of Monte Cristo is likely not only to be the longest novel they've read to this point but also, because of its vast array of characters, the most confusing. Some foundation questions help students focus on specific plot details that allow them to become more comfortable with the story itself and its characters. Good foundation questions begin with the basic details (who, what, when, etc.) and couple them with higher-level questions (why, how, etc.). The goal is to help students work with a complicated novel by establishing certain foundation questions that are specific enough to resolve confusing plot elements and open-ended enough to produce lively and enlightening discussion.

In Monte Cristo, foundation questions focus primarily, though not exclusively, on characters. It allows an opportunity for the small groups, and through them the class, to take a second—or third—look at specific chapters and passages. Soon, students realize that in their initial reading they missed the significance of certain details, that their first judgments about characters and their motivations may need to be re-examined, and that the world of the novel is opening up to them in a startlingly clearer manner.

ONGOING DISCUSSION TEST: FIRST GROUP OF QUESTIONS (PP. 1 TO 93+)

Directions: Carefully read and investigate together the question or questions given to your group. For most of your conclusions, your group will have to investigate various scenes from a number of chapters in the text. Think deeply. Make sure a character's words match his or her actions in all parts of the novel. As a result of your investigation, be sure to show support for your responses by citing specific evidence from the text. Each individual in the group is responsible for a fair proportion of the oral presentation of responses to the class. The remainder of the class will not only take brief notes but also actively ask questions, respond to the group's assertions by elaborating on the group's ideas, or add points not covered by the group. Mere repetition results in grade deduction. Notes are turned in before a final grade is calculated.

1. **Villefort & family**. What kind of person is Gerard de Villefort? In your response consider his personal characteristics, his relationship to the Saint-Meran family as well as to his father, the interview between de Villefort and Dantes, and King Louis XVIII's assessment of him.
2. During the Hundred Days in which Napoleon was again leader of France, what happened with Villefort, **Danglars & family**, Mercedes, **Morrell & family**, and **Fernand & family**?
3. Who is the **Abbe Faria**? Why is he in prison? How long has he been there? If the reader were to spend some time with him in the years before he tunneled into Dantes' cell, what would be learned about him? Besides the fact that he provides much needed companionship for Dantes (and vice versa), in what other ways is the Abbe Faria of major importance for Dantes at this point in his life?
4. **Money** seems to be a major theme running through this section of the novel. It certainly plays a major role in the situation involving Cesar Spada. Cite as many details as possible, including in the tale of Cesar Spada, demonstrating the power and the potential of money in the novel's plot.
5. **Dantes** passes through "various stages of misery"(34) when he is in prison. Discuss those stages. When the Abbe Faria helps Dantes figure out why he is in prison, what stage does he reach?
6. What heroic archetypes does **Dantes** demonstrate in this first section of the novel? Cite evidence.
7. Upon leaving the prison and during the period thereafter, how does **Dantes** demonstrate time and time again his ingenuity?
8. How has **Dantes** changed as a result of his prison experience? Discuss not only what he is like post-prison, but also how this contrasts, if at all, from what he was like as a person before his prison experience.
9. What do we learn about **Caderousse** when he is interviewed by the priest at the inn? What details demonstrate to the reader the kind of man he is now? How does he feel about Dantes now that so many years have passed since Dantes was imprisoned? Why does the priest visit Caderousse, and how does the priest feel about him? What information about the various persons in Dantes' life (Danglars, Fernand, Mercedes, Villefort, and Morrell) does Caderousse provide the priest? Why does he provide the information?

ONGOING DISCUSSION TEST: SECOND GROUP OF QUESTIONS (PP. 1 TO 315+)
Directions: Follow directions for "First group of questions" on preceding page.

1. **Caderousse and his wife**. What do we learn about Caderousse's wife from her actions during the visit from Abbe Busoni? What really happened the night of June 3, 1929, at the Pont du Gard Inn? (Note the actions and reactions of both Caderousse and his wife.) Why was Caderousse in jail, and how did he get out and why? What is the significance of Edmond Dantes' description of Caderousse at the bottom of p. 7 and of the narrator's description of him as a "wolf or jackal" when he's in Paris on p. 219? How did the Count know that Caderousse would be robbing his house? When Abbe Busoni discovers Caderousse in the Count's house, what does he require of Caderousse? How did Caderousse die and why? What are the Abbe Busoni's final words to Caderousse, and what is the significance of "One"?

2. **The missing years**. Soon after escaping from the Chateau d'If in 1829, Edmond Dantes, in various guises, visits Caderousse, the mayor of Marseilles, the Inspector of Prisons, and the offices of Morrel and Son. Thereafter, we do not hear of him until some nine or ten years later in 1838 or 1839 in Rome when he has become the Count of Monte Cristo. What are specific things that Dantes must have done during those nine years? Connect your responses to actual events in the story. Go into detail. Look at everything that Edmond Dantes does while in Paris in connection with Danglars' family, the Villefort family, the Morcerf family, and Caderousse. Fill in the nine-or ten-year gap.

3. **Dantes makes friends**. In Rome the Count of Monte Cristo develops a relationship with Albert de Morcerf and Franz d'Epinay. Why is developing a friendship with these two individuals so important for Dantes' plan of vengeance? What ties do these individuals have with those against whom Dantes is plotting?

4. **Dantes & the Morcerf family**. How does Edmond Dantes bring about the downfall of the Count de Morcerf? How does he really feel about Albert? What has Mercedes' life been like since she married Fernand Mondego?

5. **Dantes & the Cavalcantis**. Who are the Cavalcantis? How is each of them being used to help further the Count's mission?

6. **Dantes & the Danglars family**. The Baron and Baroness Danglars are apparently involved in financial speculations. What exactly does it mean to speculate in this manner? How do the two of them speculate? What eventually begins to happen due to their speculations? How is Lucien Debray involved in these speculations? What is his relationship with the Baroness? How is the Count of Monte Cristo involved?
   A. What is the relationship of the Baron and Mme. Danglars at this time?
   B. How does the Count "save" the "domestic peace of their family"?
   C. How do the horses help Dantes make a "saving" connection to the Villefort family?
   D. What do we learn about the Danglars' speculation from Chpt. 30? According to Lucien, who is the real speculator in the family? When Albert suggests that Mme. Danglars must be taught a lesson, what would be Lucien's role in providing the lesson? Note Lucien's reactions to Albert's idea. Why might Lucien react to Albert's suggestion the way he did? What does the Count notice?
   E. Chpt. 34—The Count tells Mme. Villefort that he wants to see a telegraph, something that "has made me thoughtful for hours on end." What is this really suggesting to the reader? What that very evening appears in La Messager? How is this connected to what we already know?
   F. Chpt. 37—What does the argument between the Baron and the Baroness concern? What do we learn about the recent method of speculating in this family? What charge does the Baron make against his wife and, especially, Lucien? What is he accusing Lucien of doing?

7. **Dantes & the Villefort family**. In a conversation with Mme. Villefort, Edmond Dantes says that he has followed the example of King Mithridates. What significance does this allusion to Mithridates have in the plot? Why is the Count discussing toxicology with her? What is brucine? How is it involved in the story?
   A. What evidence is there that the incident concerning the runaway horses with the carriage carrying Mme. Villefort and her son was planned by the Count? For what purpose?
   B. When we discover that the Count had met Mme. Villefort and her children before (Chpt. 29), what do the details of that visit reveal to the reader?
   C. What is significant about how Mme. de Villefort manages to get herself alone with the Count?
   D. Upon leaving the Villefort residence, the Count suggests that he has sown seed that "hasn't fallen on barren ground." Noting the conversation between Mme Villefort and the Count, what seed has been sown?
   E. What are Mme. Villefort's feelings concerning Valentine's impending marriage to Franz d'Epinay, and how are these feelings relevant to her interest in poisons?

8. **Dantes**. Carefully note the details of Chpts. 26 and 51. How does Edmond Dantes perceive himself? Under what other circumstances in the story is he referred to by others as being some sort of supernatural figure? What major change or changes occur in Chpt. 51, and why?

A Continual Dialogue

Providing a foundation for ongoing discussion, then letting go

Discussing *Great Expectations*

All discussion needs some type of solid foundation; otherwise, instead of listening to one another and responding accordingly, individuals will follow their own agendas and we'll have one Tower of Babel after another. By teaching how to discuss intelligently, we as educators are teaching so many skills that form the basis of community: how to listen carefully and sensitively to the points others make; how to disagree without being disagreeable; how to read critically; how to craft questions that go beyond the "yes" or "no" response, that, in fact, elicit genuine thoughtfulness and that require the reader to think deeply about the world the writer has created.

Charles Dickens may seem like a tough writer to teach because he's a wordsmith who employs lengthy sentences that many students have difficulty digesting. But he's the perfect writer for teaching; he's so cinematic. And using that cinematic flavor at the outset is a great way to hook students into reading the book and wanting to discuss it. (See Chapter 4 of this text for an idea of how to grab your students' attention when beginning Great Expectations or other texts.) We'll spend the first week talking daily about those things that students immediately have questions about as they read.

With this novel I require a discussion log, explained on p. 25, which is often the basis for starting discussions each day. Moreover, once a third of the novel has been read, about the time Pip has moved from the village to London, I employ the small group presentation technique used with Monte Cristo in order to have the students work together on looking at the novel's world as a whole. These foundation questions, many of which will relate to questions in the students' discussion logs, help students to focus as they continue their reading and discussion of this wonderfully rich story.

KEEPING STUDENTS ON THE SAME PAGE

Provide a syllabus ahead of time, one for students and for parents. Use a combination of testing and daily quizzes to ensure that students do not put off reading, and so you'll know who is reading and how well. Phone parents when needed.

A sample testing schedule
Mon., March 15: Chpts. 1-8
Thurs., March 18: Chpts. 9-15
Mon., March 22: Chpts. 16-23
Thurs., March 25: Chpts. 24-31
Mon., March 29: Chpts. 32-44
Thurs., April 1: Chpts. 45-58

These are testing days. My tests and daily quizzes are designed to make sure my students are reading, are reading well, and are reading at a similar pace so that all can participate in class discussion together.

Daily quizzes
Break down the larger readings into daily segments. For example, for Thurs., March 11, Chpts. 1-2; for Fri., March 12, Chpts. 3-5; etc..

Ask one or two questions per day. I ask questions requiring very short answers and allow a matter of five to ten seconds to complete. Students quickly exchange papers, grade, and turn them in. Next class day, the quiz papers are returned and used for that day's quiz. Upon finishing the novel, I record the overall daily quiz grade.

Page and chapter references refer to the abridged version of Great Expectations in the Harcourt Brace text.

GREAT EXPECTATIONS
DISCUSSION LOG

PURPOSE: To provide students the opportunity to formulate discussion questions that will clarify what puzzles them while reading and/or may help the class understand more about the world that the author has created in this novel.

METHOD: As students read a grouping of chapters (see testing schedule), they are to write out neatly or type questions that occur to them. Each student should create a minimum of five thoughtful questions per grouping of chapters. They are to keep the questions organized, spaced, and ready to turn in to the teacher. After each question, the students are to cite the chapter, page, and column (if the page has columns) from which the question is derived. For example, What does the narrator mean when he says his sister raised him"by hand"? (2: 14,1)

TYPES OF QUESTIONS:
Students are to create questions similar to those suggested for the Tournament of Scholars. (See next column.)

THE LOG AND DISCUSSION:
Once the daily quiz is out of the way, I often begin discussion by asking if anyone has a question from his or her log that involves a specific character or situation. Once the question is read aloud, students respond and then we proceed to another question on that same character or situation.

Types of questions to create for the discussion log

Directions: For each group of chapters to be tested, you must create a minimum of five questions from differing chapters that should be asked during discussion and "answered" during discussion if we are to truly understand the world Charles Dickens has created in this novel. Your questions must be solely yours and no one else's. Do not create just any questions. They must be thoughtful and be the kind to elicit information helpful to the class' overall understanding of the novel, or they will receive no points. In addition, never ask a question that elicits merely a "yes" or "no" response.

Questions should be created along the following lines:

A. **Clarification** questions: If what is happening in the novel is confusing to you the reader, you should create a question that specifically addresses the situation that needs to be clarified in your mind. Keep in mind that Dickens' novel is, among other things, a mystery, so be as specific as possible in stating your question.

B. **Character** questions: Questions that inquire into the motivations or characteristics of individual characters in the novel can be very helpful as will any questions that require we draw conclusions or make inferences about a character because of what he or she says or does. Again, do not ask general questions. Your question must be tied to a specific incident or conversation in the story.

C. Questions concerning the **author's purpose or technique**: These questions will seek to figure out why Charles Dickens seems to emphasize a specific trait or habit of a character, why he repeats a certain idea, why he uses a specific simile or metaphor, or why he creates an image or a symbol at a specific point in the story.

D. Questions that require making perceptive **connections within the text**: These questions will concentrate on how one part of the story is connected to another, how one character is like (or unlike) another, how one image in a certain chapter relates to an image in another chapter.

E. Questions that require making perceptive **connections between this story and other stories** we've read: These questions will demonstrate your ability to perceive how characters, situations, themes, etc., in one story compare and/or contrast with characters, situations, and themes from other stories.

F. Questions about **the narrator** as narrator: This novel is a "bildungsroman," a type of novel that records the education of the main character, and is told in the first-person. The protagonist is the narrator, who is looking back over his life. Questions that address what the narrator is learning, both good and bad, as he grows up or what he has learned, now that he's looking back on his life, will help elucidate the central character for all of us.

G. Questions that **apply the novel to life in general**: Throughout the novel you may find situations that apply to people or events today. Again, general questions will not be appropriate. Your question should refer to a specific situation in the story.

Small groups to large group in *Great Expectations*

When you've taught a novel a few times, you begin to see patterns in how students comprehend the text. While I begin Great Expectations with a reliance on questions from the logs, there comes a certain point when it is helpful to set up foundation questions that will help clarify matters as we move towards the novel's climax and keep all of us as readers viewing the novel's world as a whole. Therefore, once students have read about a third of the novel and each day's discussion has focused on questions from the logs, I turn to small groups to investigate the following questions, share their responses with the class, and have all students discuss them.

Joe: Investigate Joe Gargery based not on what others say about him, but on his own actions. What kind of man is Joe Gargery? What is Joe trying to explain to Pip in Chpt. 9, the chapter after Pip has visited Miss Havisham's house for the first time? What similarities do we find in the scene concerning Joe and Miss Havisham (Chpt. 13) and Joe and Mr. Jaggers (Chpt. 18)? What happens in Chpt. 18 that shows there is something that will make Joe mad enough to be willing to fight?

Biddy: We first meet Biddy in Chpt. 7. Compare the description of Biddy in Chpt. 7 with the one of her in Chpt. 17. By the time she comes to live with them at the forge, what changes do we note in Biddy, and what evidence is there that she is quite intelligent and clever? What does Pip discuss with Biddy in their conversations in Chpts. 17 and 19? What do we learn about Biddy's attitude concerning Pip from these conversations? What do we learn about Pip?

Matthew and the sycophants: Who is Matthew Pocket, and why doesn't he come to visit Miss Havisham? In your response use all the information concerning Matthew Pocket that we have up through Chpt. 23. Note the first time Matthew Pocket is mentioned in Chpt. 11 of the the story, by whom, and concerning what (three times in Chpt. 11)? Considering who is talking about him at this time, what might occur to a truly discerning reader? What details demonstrate Miss Havisham's current attitude about Matthew? Her birthday at Miss Havisham's brings to Satis House certain relatives: Show the scene in Chpt. 11 that reveals them talking with Miss Havisham. Point out evidence that demonstrates their sycophancy, their fawning attitude towards her, and that Miss Havisham is well aware of their sycophancy. Note the imagery in Miss Havisham's conversation with Pip.

Herbert: Read the part of the conversation between Pip and Herbert Pocket that concerns Herbert's occupation and future dreams (from the middle of the first column to the last full paragraph of the second column). According to what we learn from this conversation, what is it that Herbert actually does at this point in time? What does he hope to do? What does he mean by the phrase "I am looking about me"? How does Pip feel about Herbert? Why?

Clothes: Charles Dickens spends a great deal of time carefully describing people's clothes. The idea that "clothes make the man or woman" is a long-time proverb. Examine clothes on a variety of characters in this story. What are the metaphorical implications of clothes in this tale considering what we know about the power of clothes. In your response, note the importance of clothes to the following characters, among others: Pip's convict, Havisham, Estella, Pip, Joe, and Trabb.

The Fiance & the Half-Brother: What do we know about Miss Havisham's fiance and her half-brother based upon what Herbert told Pip in Chpt. 22? How might a perspicacious reader connect this with why Pip is brought to Satis House to play?

Pip: What conclusion does Pip draw about himself after his first visit with Miss Havisham? What conclusion do you draw about why he draws this conclusion about himself? Cite various examples throughout Chpts. 9 - 23 that demonstrate Pip's changes as a person and in his relationships with others as a result of his visit to Miss Havisham?

Pip and his great expectations: The morning after Pip has received the information about his "great expectations" from Mr. Jaggers, he goes for a walk. Referring to early paragraphs of Chpt. 19, what is Pip's attitude towards the marshes and the people who live in his community? When did we first meet Mr. Jaggers? What is a physical detail that is very noticeable about him according to Pip, and what might it signify? Even though Pip is not allowed to inquire concerning the identity of his benefactor, what is the evidence that suggests to him that his benefactor is, indeed, Miss Havisham?

GRADING RUBRIC FOR *GREAT* DISCUSSION

The discussion is an ongoing test that is completed when the novel is finished. Points are allotted based on the type of student participation in the large group discussions and any small group presentations involved.

ASKING A QUESTION

- a question that seeks **to clarify** events that are confusing or unclear = 1 pt.;
- a question tied to a specific incident or conversation in the story that inquires into the **motivations or characteristics** of an individual = 2 pts.;
- a question concerning the **author's technique**—why he emphasizes a certain character's trait or habit, why he creates a certain metaphor or certain imagery, why he repeats a certain idea, etc. = 2 pts.;
- a question that make perceptive **connections** between one part of the story and another or how one character is like (or unlike) another = 2 pts.

ANSWERING A QUESTION

- an answer that merely restates what another person has already said = no points
- an answer that expresses an opinion with no reference to any details that support the opinion = no points
- an answer referring to specific details from the novel = 1 pt.
- an answer supported by a specific passage, one the student reads aloud and comments upon = 2 or 3 pts.
- an answer reacting to and elaborating upon a response given by another named student = 2 or 3 pts.
- an answer bringing forth an original point of superior quality, making a meaningful connection between Great Expectations and other literary works we've studied, other books you've read or movies you've seen or songs you've heard, and/or between GE and our current lives = up to 4 pts.

Why Grading Matters—and Cliffs Notes, too

When teaching a novel, I grade everything students do: daily reading quizzes; reading tests over groups of chapters (see sample testing schedule, p. 26); ongoing class discussion, which is given a grade the equivalent of a reading test grade; and a final exam over the novel, involving some type of essay. This is a philosophical matter for me. Literature is exciting, but it must be read, and I do not wish to create a situation where students feel they can get by merely by purchasing the Cliffs Notes of the novel. I expect students to be challenged in their reading of a text. Thinking is tough stuff. Knowing they will be graded helps keep some students on task. It keeps both the students and me very focused. Students cannot so easily shrug off a day's reading assignment if they have a quiz the next day; in turn, they will be more constructively involved in discussion if they've kept up. It would be wonderful, indeed, if students would read—and keep up with the reading—without being graded; but I want maximal participation and not a reliance on a few students who always read and always talk. In addition, grading makes me work with the student individually if I see problems. It keeps me cognizant of who is participating in discussion and who is holding back. It makes me contact parents when I see a student start a pattern of poor grades, whether in quizzes, reading tests, or the discussion. Finally, my tests and quizzes defeat students who think they can be successful merely by reading the novel's Cliffs Notes.

The Discussion Quiz

Excerpted passages

Literary criticism

Open-ended questions

FORMAT

1. Each student has a copy of discussion material prepared by the teacher. See sample on next page.
2. Students are seated in a circle.
3. One student in the class volunteers to read the question.
   He or she has two options:
   - Answer the question or
   - Say, "I'm not sure how to answer this; can someone help me?"
4. After a student answers a question, another student will add additional comments. This student has two options.
   - Agree with all or part of the previous student's commentary and add further elaboration based on details from the literary text;
   - Disagree with all or part of the previous student's commentary and explain reasons based on evidence from the text.
4. When there is a lull in the conversation, one student volunteers to say, "Does anyone have any further comments on this question?"
   He or she has two options:
   - Ask another student to read the next question or
   - Read the next question himself or herself.
5. Repeat earlier steps.

DIRECTIONS

1. Speak loudly and clearly.
2. Look at the speaker, not the teacher.
3. Look at the audience.
4. Be polite.
5. Speak to individuals by name.
6. Stay on the topic.
7. Don't repeat.
8. Everyone participates.
9. Be responsible for the discussion.
10. Use spoken transitions. (See p. 32 for examples of transitions.)

a Beowulf discussion quiz

The following example for a Beowulf discussion quiz contains all three varieties of material I use on the discussion quiz handout. Sometimes I use only excerpted passages. Sometimes I use only open-ended questions. Sometimes I use only critical comments. Sometimes I employ a combination. I usually take two class periods to complete this exercise.

PREPARATION

Choose one question, critical commentary, and excerpt to include in your critical journal. Writing in your journal, follow the directions that pertain to each type of entry.

DIRECTIONS FOR LITERARY CRITICISM AND THE OPEN-ENDED QUESTION

When responding to each question or critical statement, you must accompany your comments with textual support. When responding to the critical comments, explain what the author is trying to say; then explain why you agree or disagree, pointing to text that either supports or refutes the critic's interpretation. When referring to text, please state page numbers and line numbers clearly.

LITERARY CRITICISM

1. John Halverson:
   "So there are a number of suggestions in the representation of Heorot and Hrothgar of God and his creation...the idea of creating or making, which is seen as a God-like act. As God brought form out of chaos, light out of darkness, so the king brings order to his world and maintains it."

2. George Clark:
   "In Heorot Grendel's mother's flight suggested her vulnerability to the weapons of the Danes—the narrator measured her strength and found it inferior—but in the depths of the mere Grendel's mother becomes the archetypal enemy and assumes the powers of the place itself, chaos, the antiworld."

OPEN-ENDED QUESTIONS

3. Discuss the various functions of feasting in the Anglo-Saxon tradition.

4. Discuss the functions of the various lays the scop tells during the feasts.

5. In what forms does evil appear in Beowulf? Discuss internal and external.

DIRECTIONS FOR EXCERPTED PASSAGES FROM THE TEXT

Discuss how diction, imagery, details, language, and syntax help us understand what the work is trying to say.

EXCERPTED PASSAGES

6. (110) Tears fell from the grey-haired one. With the wisdom of age he foresaw two things, the second more likely, that they would never again greet one another, meet thus as heroes.

7. (108) That hardy man ordered Hrunting to be carried back to the son of Edgelaf, bade him accept again his well-loved sword; said that he accounted it formidable in the fight, a good friend in war, thanked him for the loan of it, without the least finding fault with the edge of that blade; ample was his spirit.

8. (106) At last his part of pride within him waxes and climbs, the watchman of the soul slumbering the while. That sleep is too deep, tangled in its cares! Too close is the slayer who shoots the wicked shaft from his bow! For all his armour he is unable to protect himself: the insidious bolt buries in his chest, the crooked counsels of the accursed one.

Spoken transitions during discussion

- "I agree with..."
- "Agreeing with John's idea, I want to add..."
- "I see your point, Mary..."
- "I think it is better to..."
- "I would like to ask Jane this question:..."
- "I disagree with Mary's idea that...for this reason..."
- "Building on Dan's idea, I would like to add this point..."
- "In addition to what Bob said..."
- "Adding to what Michael said..."
- "Carrying what Jim and Alice said a step further, I would like to say..."
- "Summing up, the majority seems to think..."
- "Most of you seem to think...but what I understand is..."

Discussion Quiz Grading Form

EVALUATION

A = Exceptional insight and effort; comprehensive use/knowledge of text, original and creative thinking; challenging questions; connects literature with other works and contemporary issues.

B = Above average: consistent use of text; demonstrates analysis of plot, character, theme; asks intelligent/perceptive questions.

C = Needs additional textual support when both responding to and answering questions; clearer analysis of details needed; behavior that distracts students and prevents appropriate learning; focuses on recall of plot and other details.

D/F = Comments demonstrate lack of familiarity with text; student not prepared; few or no substantive comments.

student	# times speaking	uses text	analysis of text	literary connec- tions	asks superior questions	needs to elaborate	only plot	nega- tive conduct

three

Jumping into the Text

If an educator's philosophy is that knowledge is an entity that is given or delivered to students, that it is somehow "poured into" the students' brains, then a student-centered classroom is not likely to be very appealing. However, if an educator is teaching students how to read and how to discuss literature intelligently, then the logical next step is to have students work with individual literary works and share their visions of that work with their peers who can then feel free to react to those perceptions.

The key elements to successful student presentations regarding literature may be as follows: clear directions, a classroom atmosphere that fosters thinking deeply about a given subject, and a belief that the author-reader connection is a very intimate one that requires a respect for both the created world and the world the reader has experienced heretofore. Lecturing students about what a literary work "means" is a violation of that belief.

What does the reader see in the author's world during the initial readings? What conclusions does the reader draw about that world? As one of the values of discussion is that it removes veils and allows the reader to perceive more deeply, one of the values of student presentations of a given piece of literature is that it respects those unique perceptions gained without the intervention of an outside party such as a teacher or literary critic.

The Student Presentation

Short

Story

Connections

Once we have read and briefly discussed as a class a number of short stories, I explain this project. Since short story discussions do not tend to be nearly as elaborate as discussions over epics, plays, and novels, this project allows the students to demonstrate their discovery of thematic patterns and contemporary connections in the tales based entirely on their own individual experiences with them.

FORMAT

A student may choose to work alone, with a partner, or in a group of three in order to practice the skills of literary argumentation that we have worked on in previous class discussions. After first discussing the major ideas in each story, the student or student group will explain to the class how these major ideas illustrate themes we see in our world today. A search will be conducted for these contemporary examples in magazines, newspapers, songs, movies, videos. The text (for movies, show a clip) of the selected media will be quoted, proving that the short story and newspaper article, for example, illustrate a common aspect of human life.

If you are working

√ Alone	choose	2	stories to present to the class.
√ w/ a partner	"	3	"
√ in a group	"	4	"

SHORT STORIES (These titles are merely examples of some of the tales I've used.)
- "The Black Cat" by Edgar Alan Poe
- "The Specter Bridegroom" by Stephen Crane
- "The Neighbor Rosicky" by Willa Cather
- "Good Country People" by Flannery O'Connor
- "An Occurrence at Owl Creek Bridge" by Ambrose Bierce
- "To Build a Fire" by Jack London
- "A Rose for Emily" by William Faulkner
- "Everyday Use" by Alice Walker

REQUIREMENTS—GRADED ELEMENTS

1. **Visual.** You may produce a poster, transparencies, computer graphics, video, handout, and/or book.

   Your visual should contain the following categories:

   - THEMES What does the story suggest about human life? Draw two to three conclusions per story.
   - DICTION-IMAGERY-DETAILS/TEXTUAL SUPPORT How does the work say it? Consult your "Checklist for Perspicacious Reading."
   - LITERARY CONNECTION Do the stories under consideration contain similar ideas to works of literature previously studied?   How about The Scarlet Letter? The Crucible? Hamlet? Julius Caesar? The Merchant of Venice? To Kill A Mockingbird? A Tale of Two Cities?
   - CONTEMPORARY TEXT Choose a combination of words/lines from newspapers, magazines, songs, films, etc.. Do not choose only one medium.

   Sample Visual (without the elaboration required for presentation)

MAJOR THEMES OF THE WORK	DICTION, IMAGERY, DETAILS SUPPORTING THEMES	LITERARY CONNECTIONS	CONTEMPORARY CONNECTIONS
"Neighbor Rosicky"			
the depraved city	Cities "built you in from the earth itself, cemented you away from any contact...."	Gatsby's city	newspaper or magazine headlines, song lyrics, etc.

2. **Presentation** Time Frame: 10-20 minutes

   - Note that the teacher may ask individuals or groups to highlight various aspects of the visual, rather than explain every conclusion.
   - Each student or student group presenting must be ready for questions and textual commentary from peers in the audience.

3. **Written Paragraph**

   Each participant must write a paragraph that focuses on one idea in one story. The topic sentence is the answer to the question, "What is one point the story is trying to make about human life?"

   Example topic sentence: The "man" in "To Build A Fire" illustrates throughout his journey his arrogance.

EVALUATION

√ Is the presentation visually appealing: colorful graphics, legible lettering, organized information?

√ Does the visual contain a variety of media: text from songs, newspapers, magazines, film?

√ Is it obvious that the student has demonstrated an ability to draw accurate and intelligent conclusions from the text?

√ Student speaks clearly and slowly. Is he or she clearly organized and efficient, or is there some evidence that the student has not prepared, that he or she stumbles and is not sure of what to say?

√ Student explains how he or she arrived at the conclusions.

FOLLOW THESE STEPS

1. The group leader assigns each group member tasks: Which stories will he or she explicate? Who is in charge of supplies? What type of visual will the group produce?

2. For each story, identify what the work suggests or explores about human beings, about community, etc.. Make a list of these themes/ideas you wish to include on your visual.

3. For each story, identify text (diction, imagery, details) that proves #2. Make sure you have extensive support—at least three passages.

4. Review and discuss this information with the group.

5. Brainstorm literary connections and contemporary connections. The more variety you have, the better.

6. Gather textual evidence for #5. Write down song lyrics, cut newspaper and magazine articles, write down dialogue from movies and videos.

7. Gather any tapes or video clips that you want to use during your presentation. Check with the teacher before you decide on music lyrics or videos.

8. Group leader assigns tasks during the presentation. Make sure members know who is in charge of the introduction, explaining textual examples, conclusion, etc..

9. Students should begin discussing and writing their paragraphs.

Discovering the Poem

This assignment is a step beyond the short story presentations. Here students go beyond merely drawing conclusions; they are Socratic teachers, demonstrating their abilities to lead the students toward discoveries about the literary work.

FORMAT

Each small group is to lead a large-group discussion on its assigned poem—not lecture or provide the class with the answers to questions. The goal is to help the class discover the poem as a work of art by guiding the students and asking probing questions. Every member of the group must have a specific role in the presentation. Each presenting group will have one class period to discuss its poem.

Each group will have a minimum of two class periods to prepare its presentation. See "Group Task Checklist." Each member should have a copy of the outline and all the group's notes. Groups will present on their scheduled day regardless of absent members.

Students who are absent for the presentation will need to present their knowledge in written form.

GROUP TASK CHECKLIST

Mark off these steps as you progress during the class period. These tasks are designed to help each person in your group appreciate the poem more completely and, therefore, help your group design questions that will assist your classmates in their discovery of the poem.

DAY ONE

____ Each member has previously read the poem outside of class at least four times.

____ Each member has shared his one page of free-writing journal on the poem, completed the previous day for homework.

____ We have used the "An Approach to the Poem" form to discuss the poem, examining the importance of images and diction, repetitions, similarities, contrasts, etc..

____ Each individual group member has a written record of its brainstorming discussion, answering many of the questions asked on the "An Approach to the Poem" form. This written record includes a listing of images and diction we feel especially important to bring up during the imminent class discussion. This record may include possible thematic ideas believed to be present in the poem. Moreover, this written record includes the evidence (diction, imagery, details, language, syntax) that has led us to any conclusions. The teacher may ask for a copy of these notes at the end of the class period.

____ We have written down confusing words in the poem for which we will need to seek definitions.

DAY TWO

____ We have decided how to begin the group discussion: 1) using a contemporary song, 2) showing a film clip (groups must first receive prior permission from the teacher before showing film clips), 3) remembering a literary reference, 4) using a piece of art, 5) using an interesting question—ontological or contemporary, 6) using a newspaper or magazine clipping.

____ We have assigned the person or persons responsible for starting discussion.

____ We have assigned sections of the poem to each member. The division of responsibilities, however, should ensure that each member will participate regardless of whether the group gets to the end of the poem. To avoid a problem in this area, make sure one person in the group is not assigned merely the "last" part of the poem, which would, if the group does not complete the poem by the end of the period because of class discussion, prevent that group member from presenting.

____ Each member has shared with the group a written record of the questions he or she has created, and the member has explained how each question will help the students arrive at a greater understanding of the issues in the text.

____ We have discussed, in addition to our opening, using possible outside sources: music, film, literature, art, critical research to help stimulate the discussion and make contemporary applications.

____ We have considered questions that reflect a broader, more ontological approach (see p. 45) to the poem in order to wrap up discussion and move commentary toward a more sophisticated level.

____ We have prepared the vocabulary list to hand out to students at the beginning of our discussion.

LEADING THE DISCUSSION—OUTLINE

Complete All Parts: Please turn in a typed copy of this to the teacher before your group presents.

1. Our group will define the following words:

2. Group member #1_____ will cover sections:

   and will ask the following questions:

3. Group member #2_____ will cover sections:

   and will ask the following questions:

4. Group member #3_____ will cover sections:

   and will ask the following questions:

5. Group member #4_____ will cover sections:

   and will ask the following questions:

6. Our group will ask questions regarding the following examples of diction:

7. Our group will ask questions regarding the following examples of imagery (metaphors, similes, allusions):

8. Our group will ask questions regarding the following examples of concrete details:

9. Group Member #__ is in charge of the contemporary connection. If using a song or other print medium, make sure you provide copies for the class.

DISCUSSION DAY PROCEDURE

1. Identify the poem and author. Make sure your classmates have turned to the correct page and are ready to begin their adventure.
2. Provide students with a list of vocabulary (with the line #s from the poem) before the reading so that they can refer to words more easily.
3. Read the poem aloud. This should be a practiced reading, one done with care and correct pronunciation of all words. (You will be graded on the quality of your reading.)
4. Begin plan for leading the discussion.
5. Warning: Do not present a list of themes or answer what you think the meaning of the poem is.

SUGGESTED QUESTION PROCEDURE

1. First, read a small section of the poem. Start with questions that focus on concrete details. Follow up with questions if students seem not to "see" the basic details.
2. Next, move on to more sophisticated questions. Follow the questions listed on the handout "An Approach to the Poem."
3. Be careful of starting with questions that are too broad, i.e. What does the whole poem mean?

SAMPLE QUESTIONS

• In the first stanza, what action is occurring?

• In lines #___, the narrator uses the image of _____: What might its significance be?

• In the first stanza, what is the tone? What words suggest this tone?

HOW WILL THE TEACHER EVALUATE EACH GROUP?

A = The group begins the class smoothly and demonstrates superior organization; each member clearly understands the poem and is responsive to classmates' answers; the reading of the poem is well practiced with no flaws in pronunciation or delivery; questions are well planned and often provocative, assisting students in penetrating beyond a superficial reading of the poem; group has demonstrated creativity in connecting the poem to another literary work or contemporary culture; all requirements and suggested procedures implemented without flaw.

B = In general, the group appears organized; at times the group exhibited some minor confusion regarding sequence and questioning; more attention should be paid to listening to the responses of students, being careful of avoiding repetitive questions or merely asking questions with little regard to student answers; some minor problems with the reading of the poem, vocabulary list, and following suggested procedures.

C = Group indicates that each member is not aware of the overall lesson plan, resulting in confusion in questioning and sequence; questions remain superficial and need additional reflection; members too often ask questions without listening to student responses, resulting in questions that have already been answered; not every member of the group participated; requirements and suggested procedures not followed to completion.

D/F = Requirements not met; group unorganized, demonstrating a lack of understanding of the poem; little evidence of preparation.

HOW WILL THE TEACHER EVALUATE STUDENTS NOT LEADING THE DISCUSSION?

A = Demonstrates serious reflection about the text and thus is able to draw conclusions substantially beyond plot detail, teacher commentary, or peer commentary; explains how any aspect of DIDLS contributes to character, theme, setting, tone, etc.; articulates original commentary supported with logical textual evidence; often articulates a new way to view the text—a character, a theme, or setting, for example; posits intelligent connections—contrasts or similarities—with other characters in the text or with other works of literature and contemporary life.

B = Demonstrates a strong knowledge of the details of the text; makes well-argued comments beyond plot about character, setting, theme, etc.; needs some work with extending elaboration of commentary, making comments more precise regarding diction, imagery, syntax, etc.; begins to demonstrate an ability to make connections with other characters and details from the text as well as other works of literature and examples of contemporary culture.

C = Contributes to the discussion in a respectful manner; needs to work more on his ability to analyze text closely, to go beyond plot summary or obvious patterns or previously mentioned arguments; at times can be repetitious; needs to work more with delineating evidence to support his opinion; does not contribute much to the conversation; some evidence that student is not completely familiar with the details of the text.

D/F = Makes few contributions to discussion; body language appears uninvolved with the conversation; if contributes, comments are plot recall or repetitive; not familiar with significant details of the text.

An Approach to the Poem

1. Remember: Poetry is not explicit but attempts to communicate the complexity of life through concrete details and images that often involve figurative language.
2. Access to poetry is not immediate. Great poems demand reflection.
3. Read the poem several times aloud.
4. To arrive at "What is the poem trying to show?" begin with one concrete image, one that intrigues you or even confuses you.
5. After exploring this image, search for other concrete images and do the same.

What is the poem trying to show?

Focus on One Concrete Image

1. What are the details in this image?
2. Is there sound, touch, smell, taste, sight?
3. What do we learn from this image? Is there something unusual about the image?
4. Is the image part of an action?
5. Is this image similar to another image in the poem?
6. Is this image repeated elsewhere in the poem?
7. Is this image in contrast to another image?
8. What effect is created when this image is juxtaposed with another image?
9. What tone or mood is created by the image?

Questions Beyond the Image

1. Does this poem focus on a person? place? action? event?
2. Are there any words or phrases that are confusing?
3. What do you perceive the author's purpose to be?
4. Does the title of the poem reveal anything significant?
5. What is the tone or mood of the poem? Does it stay the same or change?
6. Who or what is the speaker?

Technical Questions

1. Are there any uses of apostrophe, irony, or paradox to enhance meaning?
2. Is the poem a closed form (sonnet, for example) or open (free verse)?
3. How does the author manipulate syntax to enhance meaning? In addition, consider end-stopped lines vs. enjambed lines.
4. Does the poem make use of assonance, consonance, alliteration to enhance meaning?
5. Any significance to the rhyme? end rhyme, slant, feminine, masculine, internal?

How does the poem show it?
—diction?
—imagery?
—syntax?
—detail?
—language?

four

Jumping

out of the Text

The Student Performance

Whenever possible, a teacher ought to take advantage of the drama inherent in great literature by allowing students to participate in the author's world in ways other than reading and discussion. Within this chapter a variety of activities require students to use the text as a basis for creating something new. In some cases, students are given an opportunity to "act out" a specific scene; in other cases, students focus on a specific character and examine him or her in detail through the lens of a trial or news conference/news magazine situation. While you will find that each activity is centered around a distinct work of literature, each activity can easily be adapted to numerous other works that you are currently teaching or are considering teaching.

One type of activity I have always found effective is that which involves students in some way with the literary work's introduction. Since we know that how an author chooses to begin a tale is likely to resonate throughout the story, having students work with that beginning in a memorable manner can often help us motivate students to focus right away in their reading and, thus, become more committed to the reading process.

Another activity that can nourish student interest is one in which a major character is put on trial, thus requiring students to think deeply about character, motivation, and community.

60 Literary Minutes

This activity takes place at least halfway through a novel or at its conclusion. The teacher will assign students to role-play characters or to be reporters who ask questions during the news conference or interview. Students enjoy acting as various characters or being tough investigative reporters of the 60 Minutes variety. It is very important, however, to require the homework preparation; otherwise, unprepared students produce a disastrous performance. I also encourage students to wear an appropriate costume.

FORMAT

1. The teacher must decide how many characters from the tale will be role-played during the news conference or news magazine.
   - I often limit the amount of characters who will be role-played to eight or less because of time constraints, but that is a flexible number depending on the literary work.
   - Students who are not role-playing a character are reporters. Each reporter is assigned to write questions for two characters being role-played.
   - Reporters should model themselves after real-life reporters.

2. Students should locate as many passages from the text concerning their assigned character as possible.

3. Generate a list of ten or more adjectives and phrases describing the character.

4. Beside the listed characteristics, write the textual support for each conclusion. (It's not necessary to write complete sentences; jot down phrases. The goal is to prove the particular conclusion.)

CHARACTERISTICS	PAGE	QUOTATION
emotionally strong	25	"he decided he would..."
compassionate	87	"he put his arms around me as I cried..."

5. Follow any directions (see next page) that apply to the assigned role, be it the role of character or reporter.

6. Turn in all written preparation at the end of the period.

DIRECTIONS

When role-playing a "character," students

• should be familiar with the "possible questions" at the bottom of this page. How would the character respond to each of them? Students do not need to prepare anything additional in writing, but they should be prepared to elaborate thoroughly.

• should be prepared to answer questions based on evidence about the character from the text, referring to incidents and traits as often as possible.

When role-playing a reporter, students

• should choose several questions from either list of "possible questions" below that you might ask the character. Prepare short anticipated written responses.

• should generate a few questions, beyond those listed below, concerning the specific actions in the text that you might ask the characters. Approach your questions as a reporter/journalist interrogating the characters. Please write these questions down, along with the anticipated answers by the characters.

Possible questions

1. What do you find motivates you in your life?
2. Who has influenced your life the most?
3. How did this occur?
4. What are your most significant failings or weaknesses?
5. What are your strengths?
6. Have you ever misjudged someone or a situation?
7. What actions should we praise you for?
8. Were you ever a victim? Did you ever allow yourself to be taken advantage of?
9. What was the nature of your power over others? How did you affect them?
10. What moments of your life do you recall as having been most painful and distressing?
11. Did you ever experience moments of happiness or hope? If so, describe some.
12. Did your experiences heighten your awareness of life or enrich you or make you wiser? Elaborate.
13. How have you changed because of your life's experiences?

Ontological Questions Questions about the nature of existence.

1. What does it mean to be a man or woman?
2. What is love?
3. Is a person inherently good? bad? both? Explain.
4. How much freedom should an individual have? Why?
5. Is a person basically alone, or is he or she an integral member of society? Why?
6. Is there a God? Why?
7. What happens when we die?
8. Is there such a thing as a devil? evil? Satan? Explain.

60 LITERARY MINUTES GRADING FORM

A = Exceptional insight and effort; comprehensive use/knowledge of text, original and creative responses or questions; challenging questions; connects literature with other works and contemporary issues; great costume.

B = Above average: consistent use of text; demonstrates analysis of plot, character, theme; asks intelligent/perceptive questions; costume.

C = Needs additional textual support when both responding to and answering questions, clearer analysis of details needed; some behavioral problems; focuses only on recall of plot and other details.

D = Comments demonstrate lack of familiarity with text; student not prepared.

F = Few or no substantive comments.

reporter/ guest	questions/ responses	uses text	prepa-ration	creative replies	repetition	costume	negative behavior	inaccuracy

A Meeting in the Graveyard

Introducing Charles Dickens' Great Expectations

Charles Dickens' novels are filled with wonderfully cinematic characters, and teachers can and should take advantage of that. Since Dickens is a challenge for many a young reader, the teacher wants to begin in a way that focuses students on the drama inherent in his plots and the application of those events to our own time. The perfect vehicle for introducing students to Dickens is Great Expectations.

Scripting Great Expectations is a fairly simple procedure. Find a chapter with dialogue that crackles and characters who are central to the tale. See the scene as a play or movie. Copy the dialogue. Include some directions concerning the characters' physical actions during the dialogue. There you have it—a Great Expectations script! In any school there are plenty of students who enjoy acting and who are good at it. Weeks before beginning the Dickens novel, have the students practice the scene over and over. Direct them. If necessary, ask the theater teacher for help. Have a few simple props made simply (tombstones out of poster board, in this case).

The first chapter in Expectations, like the first chapter in many a great work of literature, is a key to understanding so much of the novel. The two characters— the young Pip and the convict—can be performed by two students or, if you wish, the convict could be played by an adult in the school. A performance is a great way to spark students' interest in the tale, to begin discussion about key themes and connections in the story, and to have students thinking intimately about the tale as they continue reading.

FORMAT

1. Create a script for the performance or use the one provided here.

2. Prepare actors and provide minimal props for performance. Having an exciting well-rehearsed performance is very important.

3. The day before the performance, have an in-class reading of the first chapter. Assign students to reread this chapter and the second one for tomorrow. (See "Introducing the novel to students" below.)

4. Begin the next day's class with the performance.

5. Discuss the details of the performed scene from the first chapter.

6. From this discussion, move into the details of the second chapter. (See "Connecting one chapter with another," next page.)

THE SET

1. Props include various tombstones with names. Note that Dickens provides the specific way the tombstone of Pip's parents should be inscribed.

2. One tombstone is actually a stool. This is the one upon which the convict will seat Pip.

3. Pip is dressed like a poor eight-year-old country boy; the convict having just escaped a prison ship, Dickens indicates exactly how dirty, wet, and scratched his features are.

4. Keep lighting dim.

INTRODUCING THE NOVEL TO STUDENTS

The day before the performance of the script for chapter one of the novel, I introduce the novel to the students with a dramatic in-class reading of most of the first chapter, a reading timed to take place toward the end of the class so that the bell rings at or near the point where the convict tells Pip that his heart and liver will be "tore out, roasted, and ate." (Peaking an in-class reading is important.) I then ask the students to reread that chapter and read the second one, too, the one where we find Pip at home with his sister and his brother-in-law, Joe Gargery, for the next day.

THE PERFORMANCE

The next day's class begins with lights off and window blinds closed, except for just enough light to make it seem toward evening in a cold, dreary English countryside. Students in the class see a shivering Pip in front of a few tombstones and then the performance begins. Besides the exciting dialogue, there are two physical actions on the part of the convict that are especially important—that he turns Pip upside down as he searches for some food by emptying his pockets and that he keeps tilting Pip further and further back on the tombstone (the stool I keep in my classroom). After the performances and the hearty rounds of applause for the actors, we begin the class discussion.

THE DISCUSSION

Those two physical actions—the convict turning Pip upside down; the convict tilting Pip further and further back—are what I ask my students to focus on first of all. Among the many questions that can be brought into play are the following:

• What are we as viewers/readers of the text learning about Pip and this convict based on these actions? For example, for what might Pip being turned upside down prepare us? What might such an action represent?

• What relationship do we see between the two based on the convict physically leaning Pip further and further back on the tombstone?

• What is going on within Pip when the convict appears from behind the grave, and what does Pip believe as he leaves the churchyard with the convict's orders and threats fresh in his mind?

• What do we learn about the convict when he's by himself as Pip leaves?

• For all the differences in age, size, and circumstance, what similarities between Pip and the convict emerge in this scene?

CONNECTING ONE CHAPTER WITH ANOTHER

Once students have had a chance to thoroughly discuss this scene, the discussion moves into the second chapter that was read the night before. We move from the relationship between Pip and the convict to the relationships in the household: the ones between Pip and his sister, between his sister and Joe, and between Joe and Pip. Invariably, students see a connection between the two chapters. The threats and abuse and impending violence in the first chapter are reflected in the second. Students want to know, too, why it is that this Hercules of a blacksmith, Joe, allows himself to be "beat up" by Mrs. Joe, and this leads to speculation concerning Joe's qualities as a man and a husband, as well as his characteristics as a father-figure and friend to Pip. The emphasis on the physical actions when discussing the acted-out scene from chapter one often helps students "see" certain physical actions in chapter two as having importance—whether the action be Mrs. Joe's knocking of her husband's head against the wall or Joe's positioning of his leg to protect Pip.

Students will have more to contribute than time allows this first day and the readings for the next day will bring further questions to mind. You have them where you want them— they're eating at the heart of Dickens' novel.

Because Dickens so often serialized his novels, he wrote for an audience whose readership he wanted to maintain; therefore, the suspenseful rhythms of mystery and surprise that are found in Dickens are a hook by which the teacher can keep young readers involved in their reading even when the reading is difficult. A thorough discussion of Dickens' created world provides a forum by which students can achieve insights in the interconnectedness of parts to the whole and, thus, can figure out as a class what this master of the language is up to rather than have the teacher explain it to them.

Script for Chapter One of Dickens' Great Expectations

Scene: churchyard; cemetery; toward dusk of Christmas Eve.
Props: tombstones (convert student desks into two or three, one having the appropriate inscriptions of Pip's mom and dad) plus five small ones (use shoe boxes, perhaps).

Pip (alone—sitting on ground near tombstone—it's cold; he's seven or eight and clothed like the poor country boy he is—he's shivering) My father's family name being Pirrip, and my Christian name Philip, my infant tongue could make of both names nothing longer or more explicit than Pip. So I called myself Pip, and came to be called Pip. (his shivering is more pronounced) I give Pirrip as my father's family name, on the authority of his tombstone and my sister—Mrs. Joe Gargery, who married the blacksmith. I never saw my father, PHILIP PIRRIP, LATE OF THIS PARISH, or my mother, ALSO GEORGIANA WIFE OF THE ABOVE. I never saw their likenesses either, their days being long before the days of photographs. (shivering louder—it's getting dark, it's windy, he's afraid; a few tears may be emerging) To these five little stone lozenges, each sacred to the memory of five little brothers of mine, (tears) I am indebted for a belief I religiously entertain that they had all been born on their backs with their hands in their trousers pockets, and had never taken them out in this state of existence. (more tears)

Convict Hold your noise! (he appears from behind the tombstone in coarse gray, broken shoes, perhaps an old rag tied around head—all wet and muddy and clothing cut and torn and falling off of him—he limps, an iron on his leg, and shivers and growls and glares and his teeth chatter and he seizes Pip by the throat) Keep still, you little devil, or I'll cut your throat!

Pip Oh! Don't cut my throat, sir. Pray don't do it, sir.

Convict Tell us your name! Quick!

Pip Pip, sir.

Convict Once more! Give it mouth!!

Pip Pip. Pip, sir.

Convict Show us where you live. Pint out the place!

Pip (points in direction beyond church)

Convict (picks Pip up and turns him upside down—piece of bread falls from his pocket—after seating Pip on a tombstone, the convict eats bread ravenously) You young dog (he licks his lips) what fat cheeks you ha' got. Darn me if I couldn't eat 'em, and if I han't half a mind to't!

Pip (holding tighter to the tombstone) Pray don't do it, sir. Don't, sir, if you please.

Convict Now lookee here! Where's your mother?

Pip There, sir!

Convict (Startled, he makes a run for it but stops and looks over his shoulder.)

Pip (very timid) There, sir! Also Georgiana. That's my mother.

Convict Oh! And is that your father alonger your mother?

Pip Yes, sir, him, too; late of the parish.

Convict Ha! Who d'ye live with—supposin' ye're kindly let to live, which I han't made up my mind about?

Pip My sister, sir—Mrs. Joe Gargery—wife of Joe Gargery, the blacksmith, sir.

Convict Blacksmith, eh? (looks down at leg, then moves closer to Pip and begins to tilt him back as far as he can—and after each of his questions, he tilts Pip further and further back) Now lookee here. The question being whether you're to be let to live. You know what a file is?

Pip Yes, sir.

Convict And you know what wittles is?

Pip Yes, sir.

Convict You get me a file. (tilt) And you get me wittles. (tilt) You bring 'em both to me. (tilt) Or I'll have your heart and liver out. (tilt)

Pip (giddy and clinging with both hands to the convict) If you would kindly please to let me keep upright, sir, perhaps I shouldn't be sick, and perhaps I could attend more.

Convict You bring me, tomorrow morning, that file and them wittles. You bring the lot to me at that old battery over yonder. You do it , and you never dare to say a word or dare to make a sign concerning your having seen such a person as me, or any person sumever, and you shall be let to live. You fail, or you go from my words in any partickler, no matter how small it is, and your heart and your liver shall be tore out, roasted, and ate. Now, what do you say?

Pip I will bring the file, sir, and whatever broken bits of food I can muster, and I will come to the battery tomorrow morning.

Convict Say, Lord strike you dead if you don't.

Pip Lord strike me dead if I don't.

Convict (lets Pip down from tombstone) Now, you remember what you've undertook, and you get home.

Pip Goo-good night, sir. (begins to leave, turning back every so often)

Convict Much of that! (glancing about) I wish I was a frog. Or a eel! (he hugs his shivering body—clasping himself as if to hold himself together—and limps off to another part of the churchyard—when he arrives, he looks back to see if Pip has gone—and he—Pip—is gone.)

For information about ready-made scripts for chapters 3 and 7, contact Michael Degen at gargery@mail.com

*"Won't answer a word you say
long as you keep on mockin' me"*

The Classroom
as Courtroom
While Reading
To Kill a Mockingbird

FORMAT

Three chapters in Harper Lee's To Kill a Mockingbird comprise the heart of the trial scene in the Maycomb, Alabama, courthouse. As a way to observe the trial in an in-depth fashion, to clarify the various matters presented and discuss their ramifications, I have students re-create the scene by taking the roles of the three major witnesses—Bob Ewell, Mayella Violet Ewell, and Tom Robinson—as well as the roles of defense attorney Atticus Finch, Judge Taylor, and the prosecuting attorney, Mr. Gilmer. This is a type of reader's theater, with the classroom set up as a courtroom, and everybody is involved: Students who do not have the roles of major characters play jurors and Maycomb citizens at the trial. Once the students have read the chapters in which this testimony occurs, I set aside a trial day.

ARRANGEMENT OF THE CLASSROOM

Organize the seating ahead of time so that twelve desks are arranged in two rows of six like a jury box; other desks at the front can serve as the witness stand and tables for the defense and prosecution as well as the judge's seat. The rest of the desks are for students who will stand in for the citizens of Maycomb.

GETTING INTO CHARACTER

The entire script, comprising most of the dialogue from the witness stand in chapters 17, 18, and 19 of the novel, can be fashioned to be performed during one class period with time for discussion as each witness finishes testifying. You might consider handing out scripts a day ahead of time to the students who will play the roles of those various characters, so they can read the lines over and get into character; or you may wish to wait and distribute scripts the day of the in-class reading and ask for volunteers to play specific roles. Since more students may wish to play a role than there are characters, I suggest having a different person play Atticus in each of the three scenes. In addition, it should be emphasized that those students who have no speaking role in any of the three scenes of testimony do, in fact, have roles. They must become jury and audience members in a Maycomb, Alabama, courtroom with the mind set of the community members during that period of time. That's important because the character playing Judge Taylor will need good reason for demanding order in his court at various times during the testimony. Students are expected to listen to the testimony as closely as the people in Maycomb did during the trial—and to react accordingly.

PROPS

For the judge a gavel would be helpful. During Bob Ewell's testimony, the student performing Atticus' role will need an envelope and pen accessible for the point in the testimony when he asks Ewell to write his name.

THE DISCUSSION

After the testimony of each character, I suggest pausing the trial so that all of the students, each of whom has received a copy of the script—which will be returned near the end of class—have an opportunity to discuss what has actually been happening during that particular character's testimony.

• What is Atticus, for example, trying to get the jury to understand about Bob Ewell?

• What do we learn about Mayella's home life and her relationship with her father?

• Why does the prosecutor pounce upon Tom Robinson's admission that he felt sorry for Mayella?

These and other questions put our discussion's focus on the testimony itself, thus not only allowing students to digest and think about what they have previously read but also providing the opportunity to delve more deeply into the psyches of these characters. Students will later make connections back to the trial as they continue to read and discuss what follows in the final third of the novel.

A few days after the performance, once the students have read the rest of the novel, there may come a point where you ask students to think about which characters in the novel are referred to as mockingbirds in some way. Many students will, of course, mention right away what Scout tells her father about Boo Radley after Atticus' argument with Heck Tate on the front porch; others will point out Mr. Underwood's newspaper editorial after Tom Robinson was killed; but a few might even recall the way Mayella refused to answer any of Atticus Finch's questions when he began cross-examining her. "Won't answer a word you say long as you keep on mockin' me."

CREATING THE SCRIPT FOR THE TRIAL

Process

There are four witnesses who testify at the trial; however, for purposes of time, I suggest eliminating the testimony of Heck Tate in the script, especially since the most important parts of his testimony are referred to by Atticus in his cross-examination. That leaves three witnesses in this order: Bob Ewell, Mayella Ewell, and Tom Robinson. To create a script for students to use is really quite simple. What you're basically doing is cutting and pasting. All the dialogue you need is in the text. Should time factors prevent you from typing it out on your word processor, you could mark the dialogue to be used in the text and have a capable student do the typing for you. The script I use is designed just like the one for Great Expectations, pp. 50-51, and while I do not have permission from the publisher of Ms. Lee's novel, despite my efforts, to print it in this particular book, I can make the following remarks concerning the making of your script and the potential for student discussion between each character's testimony.

Bob Ewell's testimony, chapter 17

• Consider beginning at the point where Mr. Gilmer addresses his witness with a question of identification: "Mr. Robert Ewell?" After Ewell responds, "That's m'name, cap'n," Gilmer will continue with the question that seeks to get Ewell to state that he is the father of Mayella.

• Ewell's testimony is rough as befits the man himself. It is one thing to read the testimony silently to yourself; it is another thing to ask young people—who are neither adults nor trained actors—to use certain pejoratives that some would—and should—feel very uncomfortable saying. Therefore, you might want to consider a few slight changes at times. Specifically, when Ewell stands up and points out Tom Robinson, the dramatic situation can be just as effectively rendered by making a minor substitution. What I use is "I seen him yonder ruttin' on my Mayella." Everyone in the class already knows what kind of racist Bob Ewell and so many others in the story are, and besides, what the community at that time actually felt was shocking about Ewell's testimony—as the Rev. Sykes makes clear—has been retained. Again, it's something to consider; educators must make judgements based on their experience, their understanding of their students, and the ultimate educational purposes of the activity.

• The role of Judge Taylor is crucial in this testimony. The student playing the role will need to use a gavel at times if you've prepared the "audience" for their roles as citizens of Maycomb in the mid-1930s. The students without "roles" do have roles and their reactions should be appropriate for the particular time period.

Mayella Ewell's testimony, chapter 18

• Mayella's testimony could begin, as it does in the novel, with the prosecutor, Mr. Gilmer, asking her to tell the jury in her own words what happened the night of November 21. For time considerations, however, you might consider beginning at the point where Mayella, pointing at Atticus, is telling the judge, "I don't want him doing me like he done Papa, trying to make him out left-handed...." Moreover, this immediately prepares us for the dramatic heart of this testimony at the very beginning, for her belief that Atticus' gentlemanly conduct is his way of "makin' fun o' me" may be as revealing about what life has been like for Mayella as the red geraniums she cares for. Her reference to how Atticus "done Papa" reminds everyone, too, that Atticus, by his cross-examination, has embarrassed in front of the community a very dangerous man and father, Bob Ewell.

• The exchanges between Mayella and Atticus read like a play. Having this dialogue read dramatically by students never fails to produce a great deal of discussion about Mayella's life, about her potential to have been a different Ewell had she been able to receive an education, and—once they have heard Tom's testimony concerning the events of the night in question—about the awful possibilities of what her relationship with her father has actually become over the years. While there are many ways to bring forth discussion concerning these ideas, re-visiting this section of the novel by "seeing" the courtroom situation in this manner allows the students themselves to bring up these points without prodding.

Tom Robinson's testimony, chapter 19

• Again, because of time considerations, you might consider beginning Tom's testimony at the point where Atticus asks him if he is "acquainted with Mayella Violet Ewell."

• Whether you want to include Mr. Link Deas' interruption after Atticus finishes his examination of Tom is up to you; again, it's a time factor if you wish this to be wrapped up in one day. If you're able to devote more than one class period to the dramatization, then you might include it.

• Tom's testimony, like Mayella's, has some significant pauses. Definitely include those pauses, or moments of silence, in the script, as well as other directorial touches such as Tom's hesitation before he answers Mr. Gilmer's question concerning his apparently being "so anxious to do that woman's chores."

IF YOU HAVE ANY QUESTIONS CONCERNING SCRIPTING TO KILL A MOCKINGBIRD FOR A CLASSROOM SITUATION, PLEASE SEND YOUR INQUIRIES VIA E-MAIL TO THE AUTHOR, MICHAEL DEGEN, gargery@yahoo.com

---

OTHER TEACHING IDEAS WITH REGARD TO HARPER LEE'S NOVEL

1. Consider teaching To Kill a Mockingbird in conjunction with Maya Angelou's I Know Why the Caged Bird Sings, either the entire book or selected excerpts, as Angelou's non-fiction story takes place during approximately the same period of time as Harper Lee's fictional tale. And this is far from the only parallel between these stories.

2. Many students reading Mockingbird have little or no knowledge of the civil rights history of the United States. That Harper Lee wrote this novel during the decade of the 1950s—a decade when young Emmett Till was brutally murdered in Mississippi and Martin Luther King Jr. was, among other things, leading the Montgomery Bus Boycott—gives this novel historical importance that should not be overlooked. I show my classes excerpts from the documentary Eyes on the Prize, a history of America's Civil Rights Movement. We watch three segments: the story of Emmett Till and the trial of the men who killed him, the story of the Montgomery Bus Boycott, and the story of the integration of Central High School in Little Rock. After each segment we discuss what the students saw and any parallels they find with Harper Lee's story.

3. Sometime during our discussion of the second half of the novel, I give my students an overview (see next page) of 100 years in the history of civil rights, 1865-1965. Since Harper Lee's tale is set from 1933-1936 and since Scout's narration at the start of the novel makes it clear that Maycomb "was a tired old town" where "people moved slowly," facts of life for African-Americans were likely little different than they were forty or more years before.

A VERY BRIEF OVERVIEW OF 100 YEARS IN AMERICA'S CIVIL RIGHTS HISTORY

1865
Lee surrenders to Grant at Appomattox, Virginia;
civil war / slavery ends.

1896
Plessy vs. Ferguson Supreme Court decision
declares, in effect, that racial segregation is constitutional
as long as public facilities are "separate but equal."
This decision speeds the establishment of
"Jim Crow" laws (legal limits placed on the rights of black people) throughout the South;
the net effect: to make segregation in all areas of life legal.

by 1910
Public life in South rigidly segregated.
For example, in the area of education: In 11 Southern states per pupil expenditures
for white students = $10.32; for black students, $2.98 per pupil.

between 1882 & 1957
More than 4,700 lynchings—3,400 of them of African-Americans—for variety of reasons, including
"success in business and farming or
otherwise violating the codes that enforced white supremacy."
(Lynching is a form of capital or corporal punishment that includes
beating, torture, mutilation, burning alive, and hanging;
it is always done outside the law and the courts.)

1954
Brown vs.Topeka Board of Education Supreme Court decision
reverses 1896 Plessy vs. Ferguson decision,
declares all segregation of public schools unconstitutional;
this decision leads to the gradual end of all Jim Crow laws.

1955
Fourteen year-old Emmett Till lynched;
Martin Luther King Jr. leads year-long Montgomery Bus Boycott;
a decade of protests against discrimination and segregation takes off.

1960
Harper Lee publishes To Kill a Mockingbird.

1963
Civil Rights March on Washington; Martin Luther King Jr. delivers "I Have a Dream."

1964
Civil Rights Act
outlaws all racial discrimination and segregation in public facilities,
employment, housing, and education.

1965
Voting Rights Act
outlaws all racial discrimination in the right to vote,
enforcing an end to poll taxes and literacy tests.
At the time of this law's passage, Selma, Alabama, had
a population of 29,500: 14,400 of them white; 15,100 of them black.
However, 99% of registered voters in Selma were white; only 1% were black.

Reading the Bard Aloud

Is Not Easy, So Students Must Be Trained to Read His Words Well

One thing an English teacher ought not to have happen is this: Have students remember their study of a Shakespearean play as being boring. Too often I have heard students say that the teacher assigned the play to read and that they hardly understood anything they read and they talked about it just a little and then they were tested on it and it was mercifully over. I myself remember that it wasn't until I studied Shakespeare in college that I began to appreciate the playwright. Why? A major reason was because I had a professor who read the plays aloud, and read them beautifully. A great reading can make a difference and a great reading can occur in the classroom—and by your students. I think this is especially important for a student's first few experiences with Shakespeare.

Romeo and Juliet is often the first encounter with Shakespeare, and for students to enjoy their experience of it, I make sure that we read the entire play in class so that their questions can be answered right away, so that they're not merely reading words but are comprehending both the plot and the language used to create it. For students to appreciate the artistry, they must be taught how to recognize the imagery, and to do that they must be patiently taught how to read the play.

Introducing Romeo and Juliet to students who have never read Shakespeare before

Admittedly, there's a distinct advantage in beginning the teaching of Shakespeare with Romeo and Juliet. Just about any teenager who is conscious is aware of something about the play—the characters are so well known that some fragmentary knowledge of the play is somehow embedded in a person's psyche as a natural part of growing up. But even with that advantage, reading the play itself can become an extremely frustrating experience for students. That's why I begin slowly and deliberately.

THE PROLOGUE

Create a poster-size copy of the prologue—or put it on a computer screen. Teach it as the sonnet it is. Read the prologue aloud. Have the students read it as a class. Have them read it a number of times—a chorus of Elizabethan tongues. Then approach it quatrain by quatrain by quatrain by couplet. Help them to see the irony in Shakespeare's use of language—families both "alike in dignity"? in "fair" Verona? where "civil" hands make "civil" blood unclean? Help them see that the playwright begins this prologue with a focus on the community and not on individuals. Keep asking them questions about the details in the language. Then, reread it together. Not only does Shakespeare reveal what will happen by the end of the play—Romeo and Juliet, after all, are going to die—but he is also addressing certain themes that run throughout the play. Working with the prologue is time well spent, especially because once students understand it, they will become just a bit more comfortable with what follows.

THE BRAWL

Put away the books. Instead, hand out a script of a few photocopied pages of the opening scene's brawl, from the first lines to the point where the prince breaks it up. Pick students to read the parts and make this first reading simply a reading for understanding. Warn them in advance that you'll be stopping quite a bit to ask questions about what is happening. Even if it takes most of the class, do this. Discuss the punning between the servants; see if they can figure out, for example, the various uses of the word "move." Help them get a sense of the marketplace in which they walk. Make sure they begin to see specific personality characteristics in Tybalt, Benvolio, and the heads of the families. And help them understand what's behind the anger of the prince and why he pronounces the resulting sentence. This is so much a play about a community, and a violent one at that.

Then pick different students to read the parts. This time focus on tone of voice. Make students reread lines if they're reading in a monotone. Help them to "get into it." Then pick other students to read the scene again, again emphasizing proper tone. Then once everybody has read something in this scene and students are getting used to the fact that they can get emotional as they read and that it's fun, act it out. Move the desks to the side of the class. Create a marketplace on the spot. Make swords out of newspapers. Assign parts. Block out the scene. Show people where to enter. Those without speaking roles become shopkeepers and buyers. Now direct the scene and have a ball!

ACT ONE

Once the brawl is over, we open the texts and begin reading from the point where the prince departs. Especially for students who remain unfamiliar with an entire Shakespearean play, the reading of Act One is a time for helping students become familiar with Shakespeare's language. When teaching Shakespeare, one is teaching poetry, drama, psychology, history, economics, sociology, etc.. Easing people into the play and helping them understand what's going on by understanding how Shakespeare uses the language are both crucial. Showing students how to speak the lines so that they mean something and are not just drily recited words will help prepare students for their major readings from Act Two forward. Depending on how lengthy a scene is in Act One, I will stop the readings a number of times per scene: to have students read a passage again and ask them to discuss the imagery, the plot situation, the irony, etc., and to show them how to convey the proper emotional tone of the characters. In Act One the teacher's job is to teach students how to read the Bard and how to "see" his world.

THE READING TEST

Reading Shakespeare is serious business. Before we begin the play, I explain to the students that each will have the opportunity to read aloud a number of character roles, but that one particular part somewhere in Acts Two to Five is a reading that will be graded. When I assign them their graded roles, I make sure they know who else has an assigned role that will also be tested in the same scene, and I strongly encourage their coming in for rehearsal/tutorials before or after school well before the day their specific scene approaches. The assigned parts are major ones that will, of course, require preparation in order to do well.

DIRECTIONS

The assigned reading will be given a test grade based on how well the student performs the reading according to the expectations as stated below. A student is encouraged to rehearse the assigned part with the teacher ahead of time. Should the student show evidence of not having practiced the part sufficiently so as to be a contributing member of the production, the teacher will take over the part, or request another student to do so, so that Shakespeare's words and that student's classmates' desire to understand them will continue to be respected.

Students should be prepared to read the assigned character part in the following fashion:
- with correct pronunciation of words;
- with enunciation that is articulate;
- following the natural rhythms of speech and using the guides provided by the publisher & playwright, especially punctuation, and any notations on the side;
- employing tones (sadness, excitement, anger, thoughtfulness, fear, contempt, joy, passion, confusion) appropriate to what the character is feeling or thinking in the given scene; and
- showing an understanding of what the other characters in the scene are saying to your character and responding to them appropriately.

ASSIGNED PARTS & LINES

The following character parts & lines can be assigned prior to beginning the play. Rehearsal times can be set up where needed. Other parts not listed here—almost all of them smaller—can be assigned on a daily basis as you approach the particular scenes, but these are the parts that will provide plenty of lines to give any student an opportunity to "get into character." Note that no one is required to memorize a part. That would not be conducive to a smooth reading of the play. This is not a public performance for the stage; it is a type of readers' theater and works very well when students are prepared.

1. Romeo, Act II.ii to line 80
2. Romeo, Act II.ii lines 80 to 190
3. Juliet, Act II.ii to line 107
4. Juliet, Act II.ii lines 110 to 190
5. Friar Laurence, Act II.iii
6. Romeo, Act II.iii
7. Mercutio, Act II.iv
8. Benvolio, Act II.iv
9. Romeo, Act II.iv
10. Nurse, Act II.iv
11. Juliet, Act II.v
12. Nurse, Act II.v
13. Mercutio, Act III.i
14. Romeo, Act III.i
15. Benvolio, Act III.i
16. Juliet, Act III.ii
17. Nurse, Act III, ii & iii.
18. Romeo, Act III.iii
19. Friar Laurence, Act III.iii
20. Juliet, Act III.v to line 104
21. Juliet, Act III.v lines 106 to 244
22. Lord Capulet, Act III.v
23. Lady Capulet, Act III.v
24. Juliet, Act IV.i
25. Friar Laurence, Act IV.i
26. Juliet, Act IV.iii
27. Romeo, Act V.i
28. Paris, Act V.iii
29. Romeo, Act V.iii
30. Friar Laurence, Act V.iii
31. Prince Escalus, Act V.iii
32. Juliet, Act V.iii + Apothecary, Act V.i

EVALUATION FORM

Student Name_____ Character_____Act___ Scene___

Correct pronunciation of words.
1   2   3   4   5   6   7   8   9   10

Enunciates words in an articulate fashion and projects them clearly.
1   2   3   4   5   6   7   8   9   10

Respects the playwright's punctuation.
1   2   3   4   5   6   7   8   9   10

Employs appropriate tone to convey the character's emotions.
1   2   3   4   5   6   7   8   9   10

Shows an understanding of what the other characters are saying.
1   2   3   4   5   6   7   8   9   10

Effectively becomes the character while reading.
1   2   3   4   5   6   7   8   9   10

Additional Comments: Overall grade = _____

Mythology Through Song and Dance

Whether you use Edith Hamilton's somewhat dreary rendition of the Greek and Roman tales in order to teach mythology or you rely on primary sources, the following activity may serve as a means by which you can ignite some delightful interest and creativity on the part of your students. I think most English teachers would like their students to have some grounding in the myths for a variety of practical literary reasons, but when students first encounter a serious study of the tales, they are faced with multitudinous details involving names, places, and situations that can often become confused as one goes from one myth to another.

JASON AND MEDEA

THESEUS AND THE MINOTAUR

PERSEUS

ATALANTA

PROMETHEUS AND ZEUS

PSYCHE

NARCISSUS

PYRAMUS AND THISBE

HERCULES AND ADMETUS

ORPHEUS AND EURYDICE

Yes, I do require my students to know the details of the myths. I think it will be of great benefit for them to be able to distinguish Athena from Aphrodite and Artemis, to know why Theseus was so admired by the Athenians, and to appreciate Medea's story as more than just the tale of someone who is driven to madness. They will encounter allusions to these myths time and again, and I want their study to have value and to last. But above all, I want them to understand the tale itself and its possible relationship to events in our world today.

I also want them to have fun. That's why—after our study of specific myths and before we read The Odyssey—I have my students create original musical plays based on a myth. And the more original they are—the more the myth itself becomes an inspiring point of departure for their musical tale—the better. They begin working on their musical play before we begin studying individual myths. While we are discussing the various myths, there will be in-class work days for parts of 2-3 days. Prior to the performances, a one-day rehearsal will take place. The performances usually take two days per class.

Festival of Dionysus
The Musical Plays

FORMAT

Each group will create and perform an original musical play that is based on one of the mythological tales listed on the previous page (either the entire story or a part of it). You have two days to decide who will be in your group; those students who have not selected a group by then will be helped to find one by me. The preparation and performance criteria must be clearly understood and followed by all.

A. Groups will be composed of three to four members.

B. All members of the group must be involved in the play's creation and the planning of the performance. Each group must select a responsible team leader whose duty it will be to communicate with the teacher should any problems arise. In addition, provide the teacher with an original contract created and signed by each team member that designates agreed-upon responsibilities of each team member along with each member's pledge to carry out a fair share of the total "weight" of the production. Contracts due_____

C. All members of the group must be involved equitably in the performance itself.

D. Costumes must be "created" and used for the performance. Each cast member should "create" his or her own costume unless other arrangements are unanimously agreed upon by the group.

E. All lines must be memorized, even those lines of any narrators.

F. Group members may take more than one role in the play, but who is playing whom should be clearly noted by the wording in the play.

G. A narrator or chorus to explain certain events is permissible.

H. A minimum of one original song, written to a well-known tune, must be created and performed. All members of the group must be involved in the song performance, either through the singing itself or appropriate choreography, dance, or other staging.

I. Various SAT-level vocabulary words studied during the mythology unit should be included in the play's script and/or the song lyrics.

J. Each group member should create and supply an equal part of the necessary stage materials unless other arrangements are unanimously agreed upon by the group.

K. All costumes and materials must be removed from the teacher's classroom the day of the performance. Two people in each group should be designated to make sure this is done.

L. A typed copy of the play's script and song lyrics must be turned in to the teacher immediately prior to the performance.

M. Each group is expected to present a production that clearly shows what happens in all or in a major portion of the tale so that all audience members will understand it. Moreover, it is required that original dialogue be created and imaginative additions be included beyond the details given by Edith Hamilton in the mythology text. You are encouraged to modernize the tale if you so choose, but it still must be both recognizable as the particular mythological tale that is the subject of the musical play and true to the spirit and personalities of the characters. Wit and humor—in good taste, of course, and where it makes sense for the story—is also encouraged. Remember, you do not want to bore your audience. Be imaginative and creatively risky. If unsure about any aspect of your production, see your teacher.

N. You are encouraged to "research" additional information about the characters and tales involved beyond the information provided by Edith Hamilton.

O. An appropriate marquee should be provided by the cast.

P. Although it is possible that each member of the group will receive the same grade, it is not guaranteed. This is a project grade—it counts as much as a major essay. The seriousness with which you go about the entire project's class-time planning and rehearsals will be considered in your total project grade along with the performance. Other factors as well may require that individual members of the group will receive different grades.

Q. Video is allowed during the musical production only if the video part of the musical production complements the musical play and does not take the place of it (that is, the video should only be one segment of the entire performance and not comprise a large percentage of the "live" performance). At least one original song must be performed "live."

R. This is a performance. You want to create something that will be true to the spirit of the play, will both teach and entertain the audience, and will be appreciated by theater critics worldwide.

S. The Dionysian Festival is just that. Performances were watched while eating and drinking. Each cast member is to provide food and drink on the designated day of your performance. Everyone brings something. Two cast members must be in charge of cleaning up the aftermath of the festival carousing.

T. Each musical play is to last from 6 to 8 minutes.

———→ Working in groups is not easy for students; they need to be taught how to communicate with each other and how to accept fair shares of responsibility. One way to approach this is to have the students in a group complete and sign a specific contract in which they detail their responsibilities a few weeks prior to the performance. A copy of the contract is to be turned in to the teacher; whatever changes are made as practice and preparation begins must be agreed upon by the group and by the teacher.

Festival of Dionysus Group Performance Contract

To be turned in by group leader _____

Whereas the following named individuals have come together in order to demonstrate that they can work together as a team for the purpose of achieving a specific goal, and

Whereas the following named individuals have already begun their journey in quest of creative excellence, and

Whereas the following named individuals have certain agreed-upon tasks, which must be carried out in order for the group to achieve its goals,

The tasks that each individual will be responsible for in the planning and preparation for the musical play to be presented at the Festival of Dionysus are listed as follows:

Group member A (group leader) _____
Tasks:

Group member B_____
Tasks:

Group member C_____
Tasks:

Group member D_____
Tasks:

Food/Drink (A)_____   (B)_____   (C)_____   (D)_____
Prop/Costume clean-up _____ and _____
Celebration/food/drink clean-up _____ and _____

And **whereas** each member pledges to carry out a fair share of the total "weight" of the production, including all planning, preparation, and performing, the aforementioned individuals have hereby signed and dated this pledge on the lines provided below.

I solemnly pledge "on the River Styx" to carry out my fair share of the musical play's planning, preparation, and six-to-eight minute performance.

Team member A_____   Team member C_____
Team member B_____   Team member D_____

How to evaluate fairly this kind of project can be a challenge. When the group has its actual performance, I make notes on a specific form I have for the purpose (see below). What I'm watching for more than anything is the following: How well prepared are individual members of the group? How well do they work together as a group? How original and creative are they in their approach toward the myth? Did the students in the group follow the format guidelines concerning such matters as the songs, the vocabulary, the costumes, etc.? After the plays are done, I have students separate themselves as far as possible from each other and have each student privately assess his or her individual effort, their group's performance, and the work of their other group members (see evaluation form students use on next page). It is surprising how closely aligned my observations are to their own observations. The student evaluation form is kept confidential, and I never share any of the comments with anyone ever.

Teacher Evaluation of Festival of Dionysus Performance

Title of play_____

To what extent was **each member** of the group actively and seriously involved and prepared in the performance itself?

10 = highest possible grade; 1 = "dead"

_____ Thoroughly involved   Partially involved   Hardly involved   1 2 3 4 5 6 7 8 9 10
_____ Thoroughly involved   Partially involved   Hardly involved   1 2 3 4 5 6 7 8 9 10
_____ Thoroughly involved   Partially involved   Hardly involved   1 2 3 4 5 6 7 8 9 10
_____ Thoroughly involved   Partially involved   Hardly involved   1 2 3 4 5 6 7 8 9 10

How well prepared/rehearsed did **the group** seem for the performance?

Thoroughly prepared   Partially involved   Hardly prepared at all

To what degree was this play "out of the box" creatively? (1 = Totally in the box;
10 = out of the box in a logical and vibrantly creative manner)   1 2 3 4 5 6 7 8 9 10

What other elements did the performance exhibit?
A script typed_____
Song_____ Did all participate?_____
Instrumentation/musical background_____
Choreography_____
Costume_____
Props_____
SAT Vocabulary_____
Lines "memorized"_____
Marquee_____
Other_____

Overall creativity of group performance   1 2 3 4 5 6 7 8 9 10

Performance times: Start time _____   Finishing time _____   Total time _____

Grade (group)_____

Grade (individual) _____ ___   _____ ___   _____ ___   _____ ___

Student Evaluation of Festival of Dionysus Performance

My name is_____

Directions: Answer the following questions as honestly and completely as possible. This is confidential. The only other person who needs to see this is the teacher. When done, fold this evaluation and hand it to the teacher.

1. When you consider all that is involved in putting together a group performance, what percentage of the group work do you feel you actually did in comparison with the other group members? In your answer, consider how much time and effort you personally spent attending practices, preparing scripts, song lyrics, costumes, props, etc....

    (circle one) 0% = I really did no work whatsoever on this project
    1 to 10%   .
    10 to 20%   **What work did you do? Elaborate.**
    20 to 30%
    30 to 40%
    40 to 50%
    50 to 75%
    75 to 99%
    100% of the total work in putting together our musical play performance was done by me. No one else did anything.

2. Since it is important to learn how to work with all types of people in society—people we may not know, people with whom we may have little or nothing in common, people we may even dislike, people who are even close friends—and since it can, at times, be quite an arduous and frustrating task, please answer the following questions:

    A. **If you were to plan a group performance with the same group of people again, what, if anything, would you suggest that <u>your group</u> do differently?**

    B. **Again, working with the same group of people on another performance, what, if anything, would <u>you yourself</u> do differently?**

    C. **If you had the opportunity to redo the entire planning and performance of this musical play, would you select the same people to be in your group? If so, why? If not, why not?**

3. If you were grading your own individual performance and total preparation (you must combine both your own performance in the actual play as well as the personal time and effort you put into the preparation of this play), what grade would you assess yourself? Why? (Answer the why here, too.)

    (circle one) 95 to 100%   **Why?**
    90 to 94%
    85 to 89%
    80 to 84%
    75 to 79%
    70 to 74%
    less than 70 %

4. Before the teacher grades your performance and participation in the total musical play project, are there any circumstances about which your instructor should be aware? If so, please explain.

5. Evaluate your fellow group participants on a rating of 10 to 1 (10 meaning that this person worked very hard in preparing for the group performance and lived up to his or her contract's signature in which he or she pledged to do his or her fair share of the group's work; 1 means that the individual really did not do his or her part in the group effort at all).

    (Name)_____ 10-9-8-7-6-5-4-3-2-1
    (Name)_____ 10-9-8-7-6-5-4-3-2-1
    (Name)_____ 10-9-8-7-6-5-4-3-2-1

Telling Tales

on the Way to Canterbury

As students read and discuss Chaucer's Canterbury Tales, they are assigned a project in which they are divided into groups, each group on a journey towards a modern-day Canterbury, each member of the group being required to create his or her own tale and tell it to the rest of the travelers in an animated fashion. This contemporary version of The Canterbury Tales should reflect the techniques of satire and character development that Chaucer uses; in addition, the "characters" played by the students in each group should reflect a balance of our contemporary culture, its negative and positive aspects.

FORMAT

A. On the journey each member will share a "Prologue" description of himself or herself (10-20 lines in rhyming couplets) plus a short tale (3 minutes maximum) with his or her fellow travelers. A typed copy of the prologue and tale is due on performance day.
B. All members of the group must be involved equitably in the performance itself.
C. Each pilgrim is required to wear a costume.
D. All lines must be memorized, though verbatim is not required.
E. A narrator or chorus to explain certain events is permissible. If the group uses a narrator, he or she must also tell a tale and include a short prologue.
F. Each group should create and supply necessary stage materials.
G. Groups must write transitions—"bits of business," short chatty dialogues—that take place among characters between the telling of each tale; these passages should further reveal their personalities and serve as a transition from one tale to another. For example, look at the dialogue between the Host and the Miller before he tells his tale.
H. Although it is possible that each member of the group will receive the same grade, it is not guaranteed. This is a project grade. The seriousness with which the group goes about the entire project's class-time planning and rehearsals will be considered in the group's total project grade along with the performance.

SCHEDULE

Selecting tales and preplanning: one class day
Rehearsal day: one day ————————▶ drafts of prologue and tale due
Performance date: two class days

PREPLANNING DAY

1. Select a responsible team leader, whose duties include ensuring that the work is distributed equally, reporting immediately to the teacher any problems with students not on task, directing rehearsals and work sessions, and organizing work duties.
2. Determine characters. Your cast must represent a variety of occupations: doctor, clergy, lawyer, athlete, minimum wage worker, musician, blue collar workers, white collar workers, etc.. In addition, the characters must have a mixture of vice and virtue. You must turn in a list of assigned characters at the end of the period.
3. Determine the setting. Where are you? Where are you going? What will be the mode of transportation? Add this information to your cast list.
4. Determine who will help with props, music, etc.. (Each character is responsible for his or her own costume.)

REHEARSAL DAY

1. Share character sketches and tales.
2. Determine what props still need to be assembled and who is in charge of these items.
3. Determine times to practice—a lunch period, before or after school, etc..
4. Remind performers that they need to deliver their roles with energy and clear enunciation!
5. Determine the order of characters.
6. Begin writing spoken transitions between each story. Assign groups of actors to write transitions between tales.
7. During the performance, make sure characters listen to each other. This is part of your performance grade.

GRADING

This project will be weighted as a test grade.
A = Outstanding. All performers demonstrated serious enthusiasm, excellent speaking skills; group demonstrated creativity in setting, transitions, character interaction, costume, movement, Chaucerian style; well organized—everyone in the group knew his or her part and started the skit smoothly without confusion.
B = Above average. Majority or more of performers spoke clearly, had no problems with memorization, exhibited strong enthusiasm, wore appropriate costumes, and had few technical problems.
C = Average. Basic requirements met; some problems with preparation, performance, characters, script, costumes, props. Some problems with character interaction.
D/F = Does not meet expectations.

Contemporary Canterbury Tales Group Checklist

Group Leader_____

I will be evaluating your group based on these items. These have been problem areas for groups.

Directions: Complete and return to the teacher.

• **Blocking**: Each group member knows where to move—both onto the set in the beginning, during the performance, and exiting the performance.

• **Opening**: The group knows how to begin the performance, with either music, sound, or dialogue, etc.... Explain some components of your opening:

_____

_____

• What type of **set** is the group creating?

_____

• Which group members are responsible for completing the set?

_____

• The group will need the following props:

_____

• Who will bring these items?_____

• How is the group performing the prologues? using a narrator, using the pilgrims, using other pilgrims_____

_____

• Each group member knows to speak clearly, loudly, and with energy!

• Have you assigned transitions? _____

• Clearly list the **order** of performers below or on the back of this form. Who will be responsible for the **transitions** between each storyteller?

Putting a Character on Trial

Lord of the Flies Jack's Culpability in the Deaths of Piggy and Simon

Putting a character on trial can not only be great fun, but it can also give the students a specific point of view when reading the literary work. After reading Lord of the Flies, the class will become a courtroom where Jack will be put on trial for the deaths of Piggy and Simon. This, of course, is not revealed to the students beforehand, although they will, as noted in the format on the following page, be told before they start reading that a trial will take place afterwards. While the example that is detailed here focuses on Jack in Lord of the Flies, a similar approach can be used when reading many a novel or play.

FORMAT

In the case of Lord of the Flies, before we begin reading the story, I divide the class into two groups, one representing the prosecution and one, the defense. I explain that we will eventually be holding a trial involving the characters in the novel; I assign each student a character-witness to focus on during the reading; and I tell the two groups that, at the end of our reading of the novel, both will begin preparing their cases.

EVIDENCE CHARTS FOR THE CHARACTER-WITNESSES

Before students begin reading the novel, each student will be assigned to complete a "potential evidence" chart on a single character. Since there are a finite number of characters in this novel, the same character will be assigned to more than one student, each of whom will create individual charts for that character. Students will make a chart listing plot details, the actions of the character they are following as they progress through the novel. These charts will be turned in before work on the trial begins; they will provide each team with potential evidence that may be used during the trial.

Example: Excerpt of character chart from previously-read novel

PAGE	ACTION
65	Hester stands on the scaffold
66	Hester refuses to reveal the father's identity

CASE/SCRIPT

This script is due the day of the trial. Make sure attorneys have one copy to turn in to the judge and one for themselves to use during the trial! Attorneys will need to put staff members in charge of the various parts of the script. The format should look as follows:
I. Opening Statement
    Should be at least one typed page outlining the charges and the general
    strategy the attorneys plan to implement.
II. The part of the legal definition (see Legal definitions, pp. 76-77) you intend to prove:
    A. Witness #1
        Questions for this witness that attempt to prove (or disprove, if you're
        the defense) this part of the legal definition.
    B. Witness #2
        Questions attorneys will ask this witness to demonstrate that the legal
        definition is fulfilled (or not fulfilled).
    • Call more witnesses as needed to prove (or disprove) this part of the legal
        definition.
III. The next part of the legal definition to be proved:
    A. Witness #1
        Questions for this witness that prove (or disprove, if you're
        the defense) this next part of the legal definition.
    B. Witness #2
        Questions attorneys will ask this witness to demonstrate that the legal
        definition is fulfilled (or not fulfilled).
    • Call more witnesses as needed to prove (or disprove) this next part of the
        legal definition.
IV. Closing Statements

SCHEDULE OF EVENTS

DAY ONE

1. Each group needs to elect two attorneys.

2. Attorneys for both the prosecution and defense should make a duty roster, which should be updated each day. Record staff telephone numbers.

3. Read legal definition of charges. (See Legal definitions.) Separate the definition into parts. For example, to prove that Jack committed first degree murder, attorneys choose whether the circumstances surrounding the crime were purposely created or recklessly created by Jack. The definition for purposely contains two parts that the prosecution must prove. Each part would be a separate section in the outline. Make sure each staff member knows all the parts of the legal definition the team is required to prove.

4. Staff members of the prosecution and defense should organize evidence from their assigned character to use under each "part" of the legal arguments. For example, can Simon testify that a situation meets the requirements of "reckless"? Begin writing questions that will demonstrate each "part." Include page numbers of the text for the attorneys.

5. The attorneys will need to divide the witnesses between them for the trial. One attorney, for example, will be assigned to witness #1. This attorney will question, redirect, and make objections during the testimony of this witness.

PROSECUTION STEPS

- Read the legal categories. Decide the charges against the defendant.
- Announce the following to the defense team: "Jack is charged with_____ for the death of Simon."
- Outline the requirements to meet each charge. These requirements will serve as your arguments.
- Decide which witnesses will help prove your case.

DEFENSE STEPS

- Review the possible charges against Jack. Brainstorm situations in the text to disprove these requirements.
- Once the prosecution announces the charges, outline the requirements that disprove each individual charge.
- Identify witnesses that can disprove the requirements of each charge.

SCHEDULE OF EVENTS

DAY TWO

1. Hold staff meeting to check progress and to make sure each member knows the parts of the case. Identify which characters will need to be called as witnesses.

2. Attorneys begin reviewing the evidence gathered and the questions written for characters.

3. If the prosecution or defense plans to use expert witnesses (for example, an author of a critical article about the book), the opposing side must receive a copy of the critical article. A staff member must be assigned to write questions for this witness.

4. Attorneys should report to the teacher any problems with staff who are not working.

DAY THREE

1. Call staff meeting and review questions for the witnesses.

2. Begin preparing each witness. The teacher will announce which students are role-playing characters. Teams may provide for witnesses a set of questions, along with page numbers referencing the appropriate response. Teams don't, however, have to give witnesses the exact questions.

3. Require drafts of the outline to be due tomorrow.

DAY FOUR

1. Call staff meeting; review case to see if anyone has further suggestions.

2. Make sure the witnesses have been prepared, that they are familiar with the passages you intend to reference.

3. Attorneys must reveal all outside evidence they plan to introduce in the case: critical articles, etc..

4. Have all the requirements been met? Have staff members brought in copies of outline section drafts?

DAY FIVE

Trial begins. Turn in to the judge a typed copy of your script, which should include your case, character charts, and questions—all typed.

TRIAL ETIQUETTE

COURT DECORUM

1. When attorneys address the court, they must stand. Always preface comments with "Your Honor."
2. Never speak while the judge is talking.
3. Opposing attorneys never address each other.
4. Always stand and ask the judge permission to approach the bench, approach the witness, or make a request.
5. When you are finished questioning a witness, say, "I pass the witness."
6. After an attorney's witness has been cross-examined, the opposing attorney may redirect questions, but only questions that are in response to the cross-examination; an attorney may not introduce other material.
7. Once an attorney is finished with a witness, he or she may not call him back to the stand; therefore, ask the witness all the questions needed to prove all your arguments.
8. Opening statements should be free of any invective.
9. The following list of objections will be allowed. An attorney must stand as soon as the objectionable material occurs and say, for instance, "Your honor, I object—counsel is leading the witness." The judge will then sustain or overrule the objection. The attorney then sits down.

OBJECTIONS
- **Leading**: This occurs when the attorney asks a question that contains the answer he or she seeks. For example, "After Roger threw the rock on Piggy, did Jack say, 'See, that's what you get.'?" Non-leading: "After Roger threw the rock on Piggy, did Jack say anything?"
- **Narrative**: A broad question that requests an answer that extends into storytelling, which can allow the witness to include information not specifically requested by counsel. For example, "Tell us what happened that afternoon."
- **Conclusions**: Witnesses can only testify to facts; they can't draw conclusions. For example, "Was Jack reckless?" The jury or judge will decide this.
- **Repetitive**: The same attorney can't keep asking the same question or seeking the same answer.
- **Confusing/Misleading/Ambiguous/Vague**: The attorney's question is unclear and difficult to understand.
- **Incorrect Textual Reference:** An opposing attorney may object if the witness provides testimony that contradicts the text. The questioning attorney must be prepared to cite the inconsistency.
- **Speculative:** An attorney can't ask a witness to speculate or guess what might happen. Remember that witnesses can only testify to concrete facts. Witnesses may only estimate distance, time, speed, and age.

TRIAL ETIQUETTE

COURTROOM PROCEDURES

I. Bailiff opens the court.
    "All rise, the court of____ is now in session. The Honorable Judge
    ____ presiding."

II. Attorneys deliver opening statements.

III. Prosecution's case.
    A. Introduces and questions witnesses.
    Bailiff: Swearing in of witnesses. "Place your left hand on the Bible
            and your right hand in the air. Do you swear to tell the
            truth, the whole truth, and nothing but the truth so help you
            God? You are now under oath."
    B. Defense CX (cross-examination) of each prosecution witness.
    C. Redirect. Prosecution may redirect the witness. He or she may
       only respond to the questions asked by the defense; he or she
       cannot introduce new material.
    D. Recross by defense. Defense may not introduce new questions.

IV. Defense case.
    A. Introduces and questions witnesses.
    B. Prosecution CX (cross-examination).
    C. Redirect. Defense may redirect the witness. He or she may
       only respond to the questions asked by the prosecution; he or
       she cannot introduce new material.
    D. Prosecution recross. Defense may not introduce new questions.

V. Closing Arguments.

VI. Jury Debate (optional).

VII. Verdict.

WITNESS JOB DESCRIPTION

• Must review passages from the text that concern your character, and
        questions provided by both sets of attorneys.
• May bring textual passages from the book to the stand.

JURY

(Optional. Teacher will decide if a jury is called; otherwise, the teacher as
judge will deliver verdict.)

• Jurors must take notes of the oral arguments and the testimony of each
        witness. They will need to determine which side argues its case
        more effectively. During the deliberation jurors will need to recall
        witness testimony and attorney questioning. Jurors will be graded
        based on how well they employ information from the case.

LEGAL DEFINITIONS

CRIMINAL HOMICIDE

- A person commits criminal homicide if he or she (the actor) intentionally, knowingly, recklessly, or with criminal negligence causes the death of an individual.
- Criminal homicide is murder, manslaughter, or criminally negligent homicide.

OPTION ONE: MURDER 1

1. It is committed purposely or knowingly; or
2. It is committed recklessly under circumstances manifesting extreme indifference to the value of human life.
   Recklessness and indifference occur if the actor is engaged in or is an accomplice in the commission of a felony; or is fleeing after committing or attempting to commit robbery, or rape by force or threat of force, arson, burglary, kidnapping or felonious escape.

OPTION TWO: MANSLAUGHTER

1. Must fulfill requirement for recklessly under "Requirement for Culpability."
2. The actor recklessly causes the death of an individual; it is committed under the influence of extreme mental or emotional disturbance for which there is reasonable explanation or excuse.
3. An offense under this section is a felony of the second degree.

OPTION THREE: CRIMINALLY NEGLIGENT HOMICIDE

1. Must fulfill requirement for negligently under "Requirement for Culpability."
2. The actor causes the death of an individual by criminal negligence.

RESPONSIBILITY: REQUIREMENT OF CULPABILITY

1. **Purposely / Intentionally:** A person acts purposely when
   - it is his or her conscious object to engage in conduct of that nature or to cause such a result; and

   - if he or she is aware of the existence of such circumstances or believes or hopes that they exist.

2. **Knowingly:** A person acts knowingly when
   - the actor is aware that his or her conduct is of that nature or that such circumstances exist; and

   - the actor is aware that it is practically certain that his or her conduct will cause such a result.

LEGAL DEFINITIONS

RESPONSIBILITY: REQUIREMENT OF CULPABILITY (CONTINUED)

3. **Recklessly**: A person acts recklessly when
   • he or she consciously disregards a substantial and unjustifiable
   risk that the crime could occur or will result from his or her conduct.
   The risk must be of such a nature and degree that, considering the
   nature and purpose of the actor's conduct and the circumstances
   known to the actor, its disregard involves a gross deviation from the
   standard of conduct that a law-abiding person would observe in the
   actor's situation.

4. **Negligently:** A person acts negligently when
   • he or she should be aware of a substantial and unjustifiable risk
   that the crime could occur or will result from his or her conduct.
   The risk must be of such a nature and degree that the actor's
   failure to perceive it, considering the nature and purpose of the
   actor's conduct and the circumstances known to the actor, involves
   a gross deviation from the standard of care a reasonable person
   would observe in the actor's situation.

CRIMINAL RESPONSIBILITY FOR CONDUCT OF ANOTHER

A person is criminally responsible for an offense committed by the conduct
of another if

   • acting purposely, knowingly, recklessly, or negligently, he or she
   causes or aids an innocent or non-responsible person to engage in
   a felony;

   • acting with intent to promote or assist the crime/felony, he or she
   solicits, encourages, directs, aids, or attempts to aid the other person
   to commit the offense; or

   • having a legal duty to prevent the crime and acting with intent to
   promote or assist its commission, he or she fails to make a
   reasonable effort to prevent the criminal act;

   • furthermore, an accomplice may be convicted of a criminal act
   even though the person who actually committed the crime has not
   yet been convicted or has been convicted of a different offense of
   lesser degree or has been acquitted.

EVALUATION

This activity will count as a major test grade. Below are the following requirements and components of each student's grade:

INDIVIDUAL PARTICIPATION

• Is the student an active participant in developing and finalizing the case?

• Has the student taken notes?

• Is the student attentive during staff meetings?

• Does the teacher see the student working with the text, talking about the case, suggesting ideas?

• Does the student know the team's case?

• Does the student have a specific role during the performance? Any costumes, props? Outside research? Is the student a witness?

GROUP PERFORMANCE / ACCURACY OF CASE

• Has the group held an orderly staff meeting each class period?

• Do all group members appear on task, working with the text, discussing ideas, etc.?

• Is it obvious that the group has prepared the attorneys and provided accurate conclusions based on the text?

• Has each side prepared their witnesses and provided these witnesses with questions and textual support?

• Have attorneys followed the prescribed guidelines?

ADDITIONAL CONSIDERATIONS FOR THE TEACHER

1. Before the trial proceeds, inform students that you will serve as the judge.
2. Select a bailiff to swear in the witnesses.
3. All students who have not been selected by you as attorneys, witnesses, and bailiff are members of the jury.
4. If you decide not to have a jury, those students become staff members for the prosecuting and defense attorneys.

Stormy Weather

introducing The Tempest

As avid readers we understand how important a story's beginning can be. The same holds true for how we as teachers decide to begin a particular work of literature with our students. What follows is my approach toward introducing the class to The Tempest, where I have each group actually perform Act I, scene 1 of the play.

SCHEDULE

Planning Day	one-half class period
Rehearsal Day	one class day, a week later
Performances	two class periods, a week after rehearsal

DIRECTIONS FOR THE CLASS

1. You are to elect a director: He or she will block the scene, direct rehearsals, report progress to the teacher, assign tasks, motivate classmates.
2. Assign speaking roles.
3. Appoint director of props.
4. Director of sets / sound.
5. Discuss "setting" and costumes.
6. Assign tasks: To Do List.

CHARACTERS

CHARACTERS	# LINES
Alonso, King of Naples	1
Sebastian, his brother	4
Antonio, usurping Duke of Milan	7
Gonzalo, honest old counselor	21
Master of a ship	3
Boatswain	26
Mariner	1

GRADING

Each student will receive a grade based on the overall group performance grade plus his or her individual contributions to the group. This grade will be weighted as _____ (teacher inserts according to his or her grading system).

Evaluation items:
• all lines memorized? delivery clear and energetic?
• costumes creative?
• props creative? sound effective? set creative?
• all members involved in pre-production?
• group organized?
• used class time well?

IMPORTANT POINTS TO REMEMBER

• Think about taking time to open the scene—a few seconds of action and sound before the dialogue begins, to set tone and mood.
• Make sure your performers understand that they must still be in character while on stage.
• Speak to the audience!
• Remember that all your lives are in danger! The ship may at any time be destroyed by the storm.

Memorizing Lines?

A long-standing tradition among some English teachers is having students recite from memory passages from famous Shakespearean plays. What can make this particular activity fun is to require students to dress in appropriate costumes when reciting the lines, to become the character, and if they wish, to perform the scene with a partner or small group. Thus, it is a performance and not a mere perfunctory attempt to remember lines for public recitation. I use this activity when we are studying Macbeth; clearly, it can be used for any role in any play.

FORMAT

Each student will memorize at least 150 consecutive words from Macbeth. Each student may not perform on the due date, but all are required to be ready. If called upon and are not prepared, you will receive the ordinary one day late penalty. This assignment is worth _____ (teacher inserts according to his or her grading system).

- On the due date, students are required to turn in a typed copy of the lines they will be reciting. Include name and character, act, scene, and page number.
- Students must wear a costume.
- Students may choose a monologue, work with a partner, or with a group of students.

EVALUATION

Name of student _____
Costume

Line requests_____
Memory problems_____

A = Lines delivered with energy and enthusiasm. No loss of lines. Costume appropriate. Sense of creativity: e.g. dialect, contemporary setting, etc.
B = Lines delivered clearly and with appropriate volume and pace. Few if any memory problems. More energy and enthusiasm would help. Few or little problems with delivery.
C = Requirements met. Some additional practice needed. Some problems with delivery. Line requests and memory lapses too frequent.
D/F = Unable to deliver the majority of lines. Requested several lines. Did not complete assignment.

five

Individualized Project Planning

Some students feel more comfortable working on their own while others need camaraderie in order to excel creatively. This chapter contains ideas that appeal to students of either propensity. Whatever type of activity that you require, you want to be sure that it not only involves a well-organized approach through clear directions but that it also does not become a "make work" project.

The one detailed activity, a project involving The Odyssey, is the type of activity that could be developed in conjunction with the librarian, who will likely be more than willing to put many of the projects on display. Like so many other activities in this text, the degree to which the teacher presents the directions for the project clearly and the degree of the teacher's enthusiasm for student creativity will have a great deal to do with its eventual success.

Providing students options

The

Lost

Adventure

of

Odysseus

The Create-Your-Own-Book Project

After reading The Odyssey, my students are given a specific project that entails the following: They are to write a narrative that is, in essence, a new adventure for Odysseus, and then they are to publish that narrative as a book. A caution: I purposely do not allow the use of computer-generated graphics for this book. I want my students to use other, perhaps more primitive, media for the creation of the books. Some enjoy illustrating by hand; others use abstract construction-paper designs; a few will use nature's provisions—small twigs and leaves; others use the time-honored "stick figures"; some will use magazine or newspaper cut-outs. Therefore, students who aren't artists can easily produce excellent books. Whether one is a Rembrandt or has absolutely no artistic talent, vibrant colors can make the book delightful to the eye.

EXPLANATION

In a recent anthropological excavation on the island of Ithaca, just west of the Greek mainland, an airtight earthen jar was discovered. The contents of this jar have caused quite a stir in the scientific and literary communities because found inside were fragments of a story concerning a former king of the island—Odysseus. The current debate is whether or not these fragments were a heretofore unknown part of the original epic of Homer or were actually written not by Homer, but by the very same Odysseus who became the hero of Homer's tale.

What is known with certainty is that the discovered fragments have over 600 words and are impressive in that they exhibit a most sophisticated, skillful use of the language. The author employs a variety of stylistic techniques: conjunctive adverbs joining independent clauses, participial phrases, absolute phrases, adverb and adjective subordinate clauses, sophisticated vocabulary, along with examples of figurative language—similes, metaphors, and personification.

The publishing companies, of course, have been vying for the rights to publish the book version of this story. Recently, the University of Athens Press was awarded the publishing contract. You have been hired by the publishing company to put together a translation of the story from a now extinct form of the Greek language and to create a unique medium of publication that will attract readers of all ages and interests to purchase this book.

THE STORY

1. The story is written in first person point-of-view.

2. It concerns an adventure that would likely have happened to the Odysseus described by Homer as it does contain a few references to other characters, gods, and creatures found in the The Iliad and, especially, in The Odyssey. It is clearly an adventure that only the Odysseus whom Homer made famous could have experienced.

3. From first word to last, the story "grabs" the reader's attention; it is, says one early reviewer of the text, "a roller coaster ride of a tale!" Another reviewer, who works as an English instructor in Garfunkel, Texas, declares, "This is a tale that contains absolutely no telling whatsoever; every single sentence is pure elaborative showing." It is considered a literary masterpiece.

4. It is in "final draft" state. Neatness is essential.

THE BOOK

1. The book requires a cover that makes anyone browsing in a bookstore want to immediately fork over the money in order to purchase it; in addition, the book requires a manner of presentation on the inside pages that will keep the buying public interested.

2. No computer-generated graphics may be used; it is clear that the entire manner of presentation is the work of a creative individual. Your publishing company has informed you that it is not interested in anything that looks computer-perfect; it is, rather, interested in inventiveness, ingenuity, and maintaining readership. You, therefore, must decide the kinds of drawings, illustrations, or collage you will employ to add interest to your story; the types of colors you will want to use to make it attractive to a buying public; and any other materials you can select to create a unique book.

3. Be sure that you give the story a title and that you name the author as well as the translator of the text. (The student is always the translator. The author of the discovered text is either Homer or Odysseus.) Please place only information on the book cover that would be appropriate. Include a title page with the same information and additional essentials that one would find on any title page of a book.

4. You may present an edition of the book especially designed to be attractive to children, or one designed for the teenage reader, or one for adult readers already familiar with Homer's epic poem; it may, of course, be an edition that would appeal to all age groups. The text, however, would remain the same in all editions; it cannot be "dummied-down."

5. For your information Athens Press is known around the world for its creative methods of presenting classic literature. The company has a tradition of paying its "creative risk-takers" the biggest bucks.

THE PAYMENT

• You're selling this. The grade you receive will reflect what the publishing company, Athens Press, thinks your production is worth. The goal of the Athens Press is to publish a book for which the paying customer would be willing to pay 100 dollars a copy.

• For the purposes of this class, 60 dollars of your grade is based on the story content and style; 40 dollars on the manner of the book's presentation.

Other Project Ideas

WRITING

- Write a story or poem in the author's style.
- Write diary entries from the time period.
- Write a newspaper article reviewing several authors' work.
- Write a short story, poem, or play covering the themes of this unit.
- Write an essay on one of the selections.
- Write resumes for the authors studied.
- Connect current newspaper or magazine articles to the themes of this unit.

INDIVIDUAL PERFORMANCE

- Write a radio show where you explain how the themes of songs match the themes in this unit.
- Prepare a news broadcast covering news of that period or possible book reviews.
- Perform a dramatic monologue from the text.
- Make a presentation using visual aids.
- Organize and lead a game inspired by the tale.
- Lead a large group discussion.
- Write and perform an original song inspired by the story.

GROUP PERFORMANCE

- Perform a talk show with characters and a host.
- Perform a telephone conversation.
- Perform a newscast and interview.
- Perform a radio show.
- Perform a political meeting.
- Perform a dramatic scene.
- Perform a readers' theater.
- Perform a Behind the Writing program (similar to VH-1's Behind the Music).
- Perform a literary game show based on a series like Jeopardy or Who Wants to Be a Millionaire?

ART

- Cartoons
- Portrait
- Advertisements
- Design the authors' houses.
- Book review posters.
- Illustrations for the stories covered.
- Posters
- Picture book
- Collage

PROJECT PROPOSAL FORM

Turn in this sheet with your project.

Project Due Date_____

Name_____

Project category_____
(Writing, individual performance, art)

Evaluation of projects

• Creativity: Has the student gone beyond expectations? Is the project something
       original and unique?

• Effort: Is it obvious that the student has spent quality time on this assignment?

• Accuracy: Does the information or message reflect an accurate understanding of the
       material?

• Quality of Work: If words, are they legible? neatly printed? Is the project visually
       appealing?

• Comprehensive: Does the project demonstrate knowledge of several themes/concepts
       of the unit?

Description of project

Explain what concepts you will be incorporating in your project. How will the teacher
       know that you have learned these concepts? Explain in detail. You must write
       a minimum of two well-developed paragraphs.

GROUP PROJECT EVALUATION FORM

GROUP PERFORMANCE PROJECT

Student names

_____   _____

_____   _____

_____   _____

Project title_____

CREATIVITY (20 pts.)
(Has the group gone beyond expectations? Has the group produced something unique and original?)

EFFORT (20 pts.)
(Is it obvious that all students in the group have spent quality time and preparation?)

ACCURACY (20 pts.)
(All information and interpretations are correct.)

QUALITY OF WORK (20 pts.)
(Printing and artwork is carefully done, visually appealing, and legible.)

COMPREHENSIVE (20 pts.)
(Project demonstrates knowledge of several themes/concepts of the unit.)

six

The

Small

Group

→ *a collection of ideas*

→ Provide specific instructions that are in a visual form, either written on the board, on a small checklist for each person, or on the overhead. Don't rely on oral directions.

→ Groups or partners can do a variety of activities:
A. Review a homework assignment.
B. Prepare a summary of a chapter.
C. Prepare an analysis of a character, a theme, a quotation, or longer excerpt.
D. Brainstorm writing ideas.
E. Craft a thesis statement, topic sentences, body paragraphs.
F. Answer an open-ended question.
G. Apply a concept, solve a problem.
H. Tutor a student.
I. Analyze a film clip.

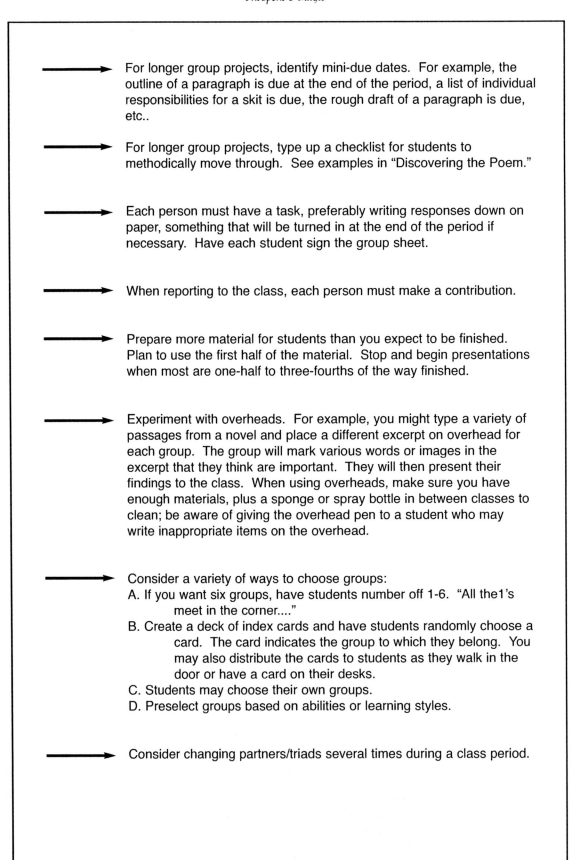

For longer group projects, identify mini-due dates. For example, the outline of a paragraph is due at the end of the period, a list of individual responsibilities for a skit is due, the rough draft of a paragraph is due, etc..

For longer group projects, type up a checklist for students to methodically move through. See examples in "Discovering the Poem."

Each person must have a task, preferably writing responses down on paper, something that will be turned in at the end of the period if necessary. Have each student sign the group sheet.

When reporting to the class, each person must make a contribution.

Prepare more material for students than you expect to be finished. Plan to use the first half of the material. Stop and begin presentations when most are one-half to three-fourths of the way finished.

Experiment with overheads. For example, you might type a variety of passages from a novel and place a different excerpt on overhead for each group. The group will mark various words or images in the excerpt that they think are important. They will then present their findings to the class. When using overheads, make sure you have enough materials, plus a sponge or spray bottle in between classes to clean; be aware of giving the overhead pen to a student who may write inappropriate items on the overhead.

Consider a variety of ways to choose groups:
A. If you want six groups, have students number off 1-6. "All the1's meet in the corner...."
B. Create a deck of index cards and have students randomly choose a card. The card indicates the group to which they belong. You may also distribute the cards to students as they walk in the door or have a card on their desks.
C. Students may choose their own groups.
D. Preselect groups based on abilities or learning styles.

Consider changing partners/triads several times during a class period.

Consider providing students with a list of group roles:

Group leader responsibilities
A. Make sure everyone follows the rules: One person speaks, others
    listen, use spoken transitions, etc....
B. Get people involved: Ask a student to read a question.
C. Encourage students to expand their comments, give examples, and
    cite from the text.

Group Member Responsibilities
A. Praiser-Prober-Encourager
    • helps people feel good
    • makes sure that each member is participating
    • encourages students to think.
B. Reader-Teacher
    • reads carefully so that all can understand.
C. Writer
    • records best answers
    • gets signatures of group members
    • hands in material to the teacher.
D. Timekeeper
    • keeps group informed of time limits
    • gets materials and puts them away.
E. Facilitator
    • understands and keeps people on task.

Consider grading students on their work performance. Provide them
with the following rubric.

Work Grade Guidelines
90-100   Clearly Outstanding: works continually on task; exhibits
   leadership; contributes positively to group; excellent attendance;
   exceeds expectations; initiates, suggests, motivates; empowers
   others to produce quality work; works the entire class period.

80-89   Above Average: strong participation in group; strong
   attendance; contributes effectively to the group; goes beyond
   expectations; rarely needs motivation; works the entire class period.

70-79   Average: good attendance; consistent use of class time;
   interacts appropriately with group; completes assignments; does not
   go beyond expectations; needs additional motivation from teacher or
   group members; works the entire class period.

69-50   Needs Improvement: does not complete assignments;
   uncooperative; needs regular motivation; negative attitude; does not
   use entire classtime.

CRITERIA FOR GROUP EVALUATION OF ITSELF

Key
1 = very poor
2 = needs improvement
3 = okay/average
4 = good/consistent
5 = outstanding

Do this for each member of your team except yourself. They will be averaged together and used along with the teacher's own evaluation.

Name_____
Individual contributed ideas?   1.....2.....3.....4.....5   _____
Individual task / performance   1.....2.....3.....4.....5   _____
Individual demonstrated interest?   1.....2.....3.....4.....5   _____
Good person to have on team?   1.....2.....3.....4.....5   _____
Total   _____

Name_____
Individual contributed ideas?   1.....2.....3.....4.....5   _____
Individual task / performance   1.....2.....3.....4.....5   _____
Individual demonstrated interest?   1.....2.....3.....4.....5   _____
Good person to have on team?   1.....2.....3.....4.....5   _____
Total   _____

Name_____
Individual contributed ideas?   1.....2.....3.....4.....5   _____
Individual task / performance   1.....2.....3.....4.....5   _____
Individual demonstrated interest?   1.....2.....3.....4.....5   _____
Good person to have on team?   1.....2.....3.....4.....5   _____
Total   _____

Name_____
Individual contributed ideas?   1.....2.....3.....4.....5   _____
Individual task / performance   1.....2.....3.....4.....5   _____
Individual demonstrated interest?   1.....2.....3.....4.....5   _____
Good person to have on team?   1.....2.....3.....4.....5   _____
Total   _____

Name_____
Individual contributed ideas?   1.....2.....3.....4.....5   _____
Individual task/ performance   1.....2.....3.....4.....5   _____
Individual demonstrated interest?   1.....2.....3.....4.....5   _____
Good person to have on team?   1.....2.....3.....4.....5   _____
Total   _____

CREATING the STRUCTURE for ACTIVE LEARNING

Classroom Management Ideas

Teachers must, of course, find a method of organizing their classrooms in a way that allows for the type of teaching that provides structured opportunities and flexible creativity. I have detailed here a number of ideas I use with my students and their parents. My classroom policies are kept by the students in their three-ring binders throughout the year. I establish the structure and boundaries of classroom organization on the first day of class; with the essentials of organization established for me and my students, instruction can begin.

classroom

policies

Classroom policies require reflection. I have found that it is too easy to include requirements that I cannot or do not have time to enforce. Decide what is important in establishing classroom culture. What are some basic rules and their consequences? Moreover, once teachers decide the rules, they must teach them to students, actively modeling them the first few weeks. Let students know up front what to expect. In addition, I quiz my students over the guidelines the following class day. I want to communicate that these rules are important to me and will help them learn more effectively and efficiently.

The example on the next pages may give you some worthwhile ideas to include in your classroom policies; these particular policies apply to my high school juniors.

www.jesuitcp.org

ENGLISH CLASS GUIDELINES

PREAMBLE
Students will respect the teacher's right to teach and their classmates' right to learn. Students will abide by all school policies.

RULES
1. Students are tardy unless in their seat by the bell.
2. Students will remain seated unless permitted otherwise.
3. Students will come prepared to class with the necessary materials (pen or pencil, paper, three-ring binder, and texts).
4. Students will keep on assigned tasks.

CONSEQUENCES for rule violations
1st offense—verbal or written warning from teacher
2nd offense—detention on same day of offense
3rd offense—options: detention/parents/guardian notified
• a student who chooses to skip a detention will serve an additional detention plus the consequences for a third offense.

GRADES
• Major (50%): tests, papers, projects
• Quizzes (30%): vocabulary, reading, discussion
• Homework (10%)
• Participation (10%)
With regard to classroom participation, each of you will begin the quarter with an average grade of 75, which will go up or down based on your behavior choices. I will note on a daily basis these choices (i.e. actively discussing the text; helping other students with assigned tasks; asking questions; any violation of classroom or school rules).

SEMESTER GRADE COMPUTATION
• Quarter one/two (80%) + final exam (20%)

TEACHER AVAILABILITY
I will be available before and after school. A student must sign up on the sheet placed on my office door for an appointment. This is an opportunity to discuss work problems, conference papers, make up quizzes, and take exams. In order to devote our entire class time to all students, I cannot discuss these personal concerns with you during class. I am more prepared to give students my complete attention outside of class.

HOMEWORK, TESTS, QUIZZES, ETC.

Make-Up Work

1. Make-up work is the responsibility of the student. He or she must sign up for an appointment outside of class to discuss and make up work. If a student fails to appear for a scheduled appointment, he or she will receive a zero for the work missed.
2. Students have three days in which to make arrangements to complete missed work.
3. If a student misses class but is present for the remainder of the school day, he or she must, by the end of the day, make up a daily quiz or turn in work that was due.
4. Work is late when the student
   • is present but does not turn in work before the tardy bell,
   • exceeds the arranged make-up time after an absence,
   • does not arrange make-up before a school-sponsored activity, or
   • breaks an appointment for make-up.
5. The penalty for late work is 10 points per grade per day; after the third day, work is not accepted. (Note: Work turned in one period late is one day late.)

Compositions

1. May be revised for an additional 10 points. A conference is required before a student begins revision.
2. Papers are due regardless of whether the student attends school. Late penalties will begin the day after the due date. (Note: Ten points per day are deducted from the content grade and from the style grade.)
3. When students revise their papers, they may receive a lower grade if they do not adequately revise the paper.
4. Unless otherwise stated, papers, tests, and semester exams represent the intellectual work of an individual student; students may not work together generating the idea, the organization, or the implementation of a topic. If a student shares a thesis statement and/or major topic sentences, he will not receive a passing grade.
5. Please refer to the writing text for sample paragraphs and papers, grading rubrics, and general paper assignment directions, which should always be followed unless instructed otherwise.

THREE-RING BINDER

A student's binder will have five divided sections clearly labeled:
1. Reference: class guidelines, reference handouts, etc.
2. Critical Journal: daily writing activities
3. Writing: essays, paragraphs, written exercises, grammar, etc.
4. Literature: notes, quizzes, tests
5. Vocabulary: definitions, tests, reviews

• Students need a cover sheet inside the binder: name, class period, teacher.
• Students will be expected to keep their binder with them for each English class period and to have it ready to turn in near the conclusion of each grading period.
• Does the student need dividers and tabs? YES! Students may not substitute plain or colored paper for dividers and tabs. Papers must be placed in the rings of the binder, not in a folder. A binder without appropriate dividers and tabs will not be accepted.

STUDENT RESPONSIBILITIES

• It is the student's responsibility to make an appointment with the teacher to discuss work missed due to absences.
• It is the student's responsibility to make an appointment with the teacher to discuss material that is confusing.
• It is the student's responsibility to show up for an appointment. If he or she is unable to make the appointment, prior notification, if possible, is required. Canceled appointments without notification will result in no credit for that specific make-up assignment.

TEACHER RESPONSIBILITIES

• It is the teacher's responsibility to present material in a manner that will help students develop skills needed for college.
• It is the teacher's responsibility to provide students with opportunities to succeed: major paper revision option; binder grade; appointments before and after school; clear directions and examples; tutoring.
• It is the teacher's responsibility to provide time outside of class to tutor and to explain further any confusing material.
• It is the teacher's responsibility to create a positive classroom environment based on mutual respect for learning.

GENERAL COMMENTS

The junior year of English, perhaps the most important year, is about choice, as well as the consequences that follow decisions. For example, a student must choose whether to excel in this class; he or she must choose whether to sharpen those skills necessary for success outside of school: reading, writing, speaking, listening, and thinking. I have already made some choices that affect students—my choices to teach high school students, to help them experience academic success, to help them become prepared for college or employment. But students must choose to take advantage of this situation. The consequences of every choice students make in this class—whether it be reading the novels, revising an essay, participating in group discussion—will result in success or mediocrity.

PARTNERSHIP FOR SUCCESS

This document also serves as a contract between teacher, student and, parent/ guardian. Success will result from this trio working toward one goal: preparing the student to serve as an honorable and successful citizen.

We have discussed and understood the requirements and expectations stated in this document.

_____
Student signature

_____
Parent/guardian signature

Thank You!

Michael Degen

Please return this sheet to Mr. Degen.

three-ring

binder

Since I require students to keep a binder with specific sections, I give them a grade for how well they keep it organized. I collect binders once or twice a semester to do this and to ensure that students maintain them properly. This assignment provides an opportunity not only to teach essential organizational skills, but also to provide a straightforward means of helping students improve their grades. In addition, overall classroom order improves when I can count on students having certain papers placed in certain sections and readily available should we need to use any of them during class.

This becomes one the most important texts for my students as it is a repository for information that students will be using throughout the year. The example that follows demonstrates what the English I class is expected to have in its three-ring binders by the time of the first grading period. For this class, the five sections are Writing, Grammar/Mechanics, Literature, SAT Vocabulary, and Writer's Notebook. Students are given the grading sheet; they fill it out and turn it back in to me with their binder. I check the sheet and selected parts of the binder. My students know I am serious about their being organized. It does not take long to figure out which students need some one-on-one assistance and encouragement with their organizational skills.

BINDER FOR HONORS ENGLISH 1
first grading period

Directions: If you have the particular paper in the proper order, mark a Y for YES; if you do not have a particular paper in the proper order, mark an N for NO.

1. Five dividers with tabs, each properly identified and spelled correctly_____
2. Cover sheet_____
3. Classroom Rules and Procedures sheet_____

4. **WRITING** section: (The divider comes before the papers that follow)
     1. Revision/editing key_____
     2. Vivid verbs_____
     3. Showing writing: fear/Assignment 1_____
     4. Showing writing: elaboration of object/Assignment 2_____
     5. Showing writing: athlete is exhausted/Assignment 3 _____
     6. Showing writing: ordinary action/Assignment 4_____
     7. Graded revision/final draft of one showing composition_____
     8. Showing-telling essay introduction_____
     9. Sample body paragraph/Sample conclusion for essay_____
     10. Internal transitions/Useful transitions_____
     11. Persuasive essay _____

6. **GRAMMAR/MECHANICS** section:
     1. Working with subordinate clauses_____
     2. HW: Combining sentences using adverb subordinate clauses_____
     3. Using conjunctive adverbs_____
     4. HW: Sentence combining using present participial phrases_____
     5. Present and past participles _____
     6. Test: The Wonderful World of Participial Phrases _____
     7. Appositives _____
     8. Using colons/semicolons_____
     9. Using commas: Compound Sentences or Compound Parts of a Sentence?_____
     10. Adjective subordinate clauses _____

7. **LITERATURE** section:
     1. Heroic archetypes_____
     2. Mythology reading schedule_____
     3. Mythology test #1 w/ all errors corrected (Gods, Creation, Prometheus)_____
     4. Mythology test #2 w/ all errors corrected (Golden Fleece)_____
     5. Mythology test #3 w/ all errors corrected (Theseus/Hercules)_____
     6. Mythology test #4 w/ all errors corrected (Cupid and Psyche)_____
     7. Mythology test #5 w/ all errors corrected (Perseus/Atalanta)_____
     8. The Iliad/Trojan War Test #1 w/ all errors corrected_____
     9. The Iliad/Trojan War Test #2 w/ all errors corrected_____

8. **SAT VOCABULARY** section: _____ words (numbered and dated)_____
     SAT vocabulary quiz 1_____
     SAT vocabulary quiz 2_____

8. **WRITER'S NOTEBOOK** section: _____

9. Citations _____

academic

contract

I created this contract as an insurance policy for each student. It allows me to be flexible in a formal fashion when dealing with adolescents, knowing that they do make mistakes and that it is appropriate to provide a reasonable means of mitigating the consequence. They can, however, only use the contract once during the year. I remind them of this fact when they are about to consider using it for an assignment.

ACADEMIC CONTRACT

PURPOSE
This contract temporarily suspends the late work policy. It allows a student either to make up assignments he or she never completed or to turn in an assignment he or she completed but forgot to hand in; these assignments would normally be given a grade of a zero.

GENERAL POLICIES
• It is the student's responsibility to make an appointment with the teacher to discuss missed work due to absences;
• It is the student's responsibility to show up for an appointment. If he or she is unable to make the appointment, prior notification, if possible, is required. Canceled appointments without notification will result in no credit for that specific make-up assignment;
• Remember the normal late work policy: Students have three days to complete work unless otherwise arranged with the teacher; and
• Late penalty for work:
Day 1=10 points. Day 2=20 points. Day 3=30 points. Day 4=work not accepted.

Work to Make Up   **Date of Appointment**
1.
2.
3.
4.
5.

Late Assignments
1.
2.

Void
• All work shall be completed by_____; otherwise, this contract is void.

Provisions
• Once the student uses this contract, he or she may not use it again for the remainder of the year.
• A penalty of 30 points will be subtracted from each assignment.

I/We understand and accept the details contained in this contract.

Date_____

_____   _____   _____
Parent signature   **Student signature**   **Teacher signature**

parent

tip

sheet

I use this sheet for parent-teacher conferences. In addition, I sometimes conduct my own "Parent Day," in which I explain to parents how the class is structured and what they can expect from their son or daughter. We are all in this together, and parents are looking for ideas to help their children be successful. I have this information on my web site, too: www.flash.net/~mdegen.

TIPS FOR PARENTS

GUIDE FOR SUCCESS
IN MR. DEGEN'S ENGLISH CLASS

1. USE RESOURCES.
• Crafting Expository Argument, our writing manual, contains my expectations for written work. Your child should be familiar with the sample paragraphs and papers, and he or she should try to model these. In addition, when students see my editing marks on their papers, they can get help in chapter two of the manual, where I have provided ways to correct the mistakes indicated by each editing symbol. Moreover, in the manual's appendix, students should follow the general paper directions.

• MR. DEGEN'S APPOINTMENT SCHEDULE.
I am available for paper conferences and making up work. I arrive in my office around 6:30 am and remain until 4 pm.

2. REVISE ALL WRITTEN WORK.
• All major essay tests and papers can be revised. These grades account for 50 percent of your child's grade. The student has an opportunity to raise his grade by 10 points. The student must schedule a conference before revising.

3. PREPARE FOR WEEKLY VOCABULARY QUIZZES.
• Vocabulary and reading quizzes represent 30 percent of your child's grade. These occur every Friday that we are in school for five days. Many students make index flash cards to help.

4. PREPARE FOR READING QUIZZES.
• Reading and vocabulary quizzes represent 30 percent of your child's grade. Whenever the student has a reading assignment, he or she should always expect a quiz the following day.

5. UNDERSTAND THE GRADING STRUCTURE.

50%	Written work: tests and papers
30%	Quizzes: vocabulary and reading
10%	Homework: graded on effort
10%	Participation

6. KNOW THE POPULAR EXCUSES AND THEIR ANSWERS.

• "No one gets an A in Degen's class!" Not true. In the past five years, the statistical breakdown of grades has been as follows:

A's=15-20%, B's=50-60%, C's=10-20, D's/F's=1-5%

In addition, because of the way grades are structured, a student does not need to write A papers in order to get an A in the class.

• "I don't know what he wants!" Has he scheduled a revision conference? Has he referred carefully to his writing manual—chapter two, especially where the editing symbols are explained?

• "He's too busy. I can't get an appointment." Mr. Degen arrives at 6:30am. If students wait until the final week of a revision deadline, they'll have difficulty getting an appointment. Try to think ahead. Students have at least four weeks to revise a paper.

• "The quizzes are too hard. I don't understand what I'm reading." Students are welcome to see me before classes begin—in the morning to discuss reading questions. Again, if you need help, arrange your schedule to seek it. See #7.

7. PRACTICE EFFECTIVE READING STRATEGIES.

• Very carefully read a portion of the novel every night, therefore never allowing oneself to fall behind in the reading; before and after reading, one needs to consult the bookmarks provided.

• Mark lightly in pencil any passages that remain confusing so that the reader can ask a peer and/or the teacher about those passages in class discussion or during tutoring sessions.

• Communicate with the text as one reads it; for example, What is the main character doing in this chapter? What is happening to the character? What important information has the character learned? Who is this character meeting? To whom is the character talking? What is the nature of their conversation? What is the main character's attitude? What is the other character's attitude? Have these attitudes changed over the course of the tale? How do the events of this chapter relate to events in previous chapters?

• Observe whenever a character appears for the first time; ask What is this person like? What is his or her relationship to the main character? What is the main character's attitude toward this character?

• Keep in mind any patterns that develop in the story: a character's actions, a symbol reoccurring, imagery repeating, allusions to the Bible or other works of literature or history; sagacious readers will be patient, realizing there is often more than meets the eye to any character and/or situation and that the knowledge needed to understand most things about that person or event often comes gradually rather than all at once.

Appointment sign-up sheet

I like to publicly post the times at which I am able to meet with students. I place this on my office door. It then becomes the student's responsibility to sign up to see me or to make up work. This also allows me to communicate with parents more effectively. For example, some parents will call and ask if their child has signed up to see me. I also teach students that it is not necessary to ask me a minute before class, "When can I make up...." I just remind them that they can sign up for an appointment.

MR. DEGEN'S APPOINTMENTS

A = I need 15 minutes to discuss a matter with the teacher.
Q = I only need to come in and make up a quiz or test.

	MONDAY	TUESDAY	WEDNESDAY	THURSDAY	FRIDAY
7:10	student gov.	A:	A:	A:	A:
		Q:	Q:	Q:	Q:
7:25	student gov.	A:	A:	A:	A:
		Q:	Q:	Q:	Q:
7:40	student gov.	A:	A:	A:	A:
		Q:	Q:	Q:	Q:
period 1	A:	A:	A:	A:	A:
	Q:	Q:	Q:	Q:	Q:
	A:	A:	A:	A:	A:
period 2	class	class	class	class	class
period 3	A:	A:	A:	A:	A:
	Q:	Q:	Q:	Q:	Q:
	A:	A:	A:	A:	A:
period 4	class	class	class	class	class
period 5	A:	A:	A:	A:	A:
	Q:	Q:	Q:	Q:	Q:
	A:	A:	A:	A:	A:
period 6	class	class	class	class	class
period 7	class	class	class	class	class
period 8	class	class	class	class	class
3:30	A:	A:	A:	A:	A:
	Q:	Q:	Q:	Q:	Q:
	Q:	Q:	Q:	Q:	Q:
3:45	A:	A:	A:	A:	A:
	Q:	Q:	Q:	Q:	Q:
	Q:	Q:	Q:	Q:	Q:
4:00	A:	A:	A:	A:	A:
	A.	A.	A.	A.	A.
	A.	A.	A.	A.	A.

CREATING

The

If you are teaching a novel that, because of various factors—extremely sophisticated vocabulary; lengthy, quite complex sentence structures; a vast assortment of characters— causes many students to give up before they get very far in the reading of it, you might consider creating reading bookmarks for your students. Each bookmark covers a specific grouping of chapters and, when students are taught how to use

Bookmark

them prior to and after reading a chapter, can be very beneficial. I show my students how to read over the chapter notations on the bookmark before they read the chapter; this helps them focus on specific points that I know will be important in their understanding of the novel. After they read the chapter, I tell them to review those bookmark notations and make sure that they did not miss any of those features. Whenever I give daily reading quizzes and my students have bookmarks, I know that the bookmarks will be the source of my quiz questions.

What follows is a sample reading bookmark for the first eight chapters of Great Expectations. For more information about bookmarks, contact Michael Degen at gargery@yahoo.com.

GREAT EXPECTATIONS
BOOKMARK CHAPTERS 1 TO 8

1—Reread this chapter. As we meet Pip for the first time, observe what Pip is learning about himself in this graveyard. • Focus, as well, on physical details concerning both Pip and the convict • Pip's 7 or 8-year-old reaction to the convict • what he sees when he sees the convict • how trustworthy Pip is likely to be as an observer of the reality of his situation • the possible motivations of the convict in acting the way he does toward Pip • the last image we have of the convict in this chapter and what it might suggest about him.

2—Pip at home with his family: Observe the relationship between Pip and his sister as well as the relationship between Pip and Joe • the married life of the Gargery couple • the day and the season of the year • and the Hulks.

3—Pip and the convicts. Observe Pip and "his" convict • how their relationship develops • any physical actions on the convict's part which show us something about him.

4—The Christmas dinner: Meet the guests • and pay close attention to Pumblechook and Wopsle • to Pip's feelings and concerns • to the stone bottle.

5—The convicts in the marshes: Reread what the two convicts say about each other to the soldiers, especially what Pip's convict has to say. • Observe Pip's convict's motivations in doing what he does with the other convict • and physical actions on Pip's convict's part during this scene • and Pip's convict's confession before he's taken away.

6—Pip and Joe. Follow their relationship closely. • Then observe how it changes throughout the story • and what causes it to change.

7—Pip and his sister and money. • Pip's education • Observe what we learn about Biddy • about Pip's developing relationship with Joe throughout this chapter • what we learn about Joe, the kind of man he is, about Joe's parents, what he experienced as a child • and what he explains to Pip about his relationship to his wife, the Mrs. Joe.

8—Pip's visit to Satis House. Observe physical details concerning the house, the rooms, and Mrs. Havisham • note the reason for Pip being there • the relationship between Mrs. Havisham and Estella • the relationship between Estella and Pip • Pip's walk home • what is Pip thinking about on his way home?

Other texts of interest from Telemachos Publishing

A COMPOSITION TEXT PERFECT FOR THE TEACHER AND EACH STUDENT!

Crafting Expository Argument

Practical Approaches to the Writing Process for Students & Teachers

Fourth Edition
Extensively Revised!

Michael Degen

DISCOVER INSIDE
Universal writing skills development that teaches students
- how to craft a well-organized expository essay, including
- how to formulate precise thesis statements and topic sentences
- how to create attention-grabbing introductions and thoughtful conclusions
- how to elaborate each concrete detail extensively
- how to tie ideas together with coherent transitions
- how to blend their words smoothly with direct quotations
- how to compose elegant sentences that contain a wide variety of sophisticated structures
- how to revise their work for improved quality.

Resources that students and teachers can use:
- student-written model paragraphs and essays, annotated
- a clear method for understanding and using in their writing the primary structures of the sentence—the clause and the phrase
- sentence combining and other structure exercises
- MLA documentation rules
- glossary of literary terms
- editing symbols that address the problems of young writers: elaboration, coherence, organization, style, etc..

A suggested lesson planning sequence that weaves grammar instruction with the writing process for an entire school year.

INCLUDES

Grammar for Structure and Syntax: The Fusion of Grammar Instruction with the Writing Process

Appropriate for grades 9-12 AP, IB, honors, and regular English students

The Telemachos Workshops

Workshop 1 re writing methodologies
Workshop 2 re grammar instruction during the writing process
Workshop 3 re active learning strategies for reading literature

for teachers of
Grades 7-12
Regular, AP, IB, Honors
English students
*one-and-a-half hour, three hour,
and six hour workshops offered*

Workshop 1
FOCUS ONE
Teaching the Essay
or FOCUS TWO
Teaching the Paragraph
or FOCUS THREE
Developing Writing Skills

The strategies involved not only address AP and IB objectives, but also those composition elements required on statewide tests for all levels of students as they develop fundamental writing skills: extensively elaborating ideas, using vivid verbs, focusing on concrete detail, improving coherence, varying sentence style, and organizing information both within paragraphs and larger papers. Teachers will receive evaluation rubrics for making grading more objective and efficient, and the detailed lesson plans that are shaped around four basic teaching principles: clear directions, repetition, revision, and modeling.

Workshop 2
**Weaving
Grammar Instruction
into the Writing Process**

The debate between grammar traditionalists and grammar heathens is pointless: We write using grammatical structures, and we need to help our students understand the structures of the language and how to manipulate them. The question is how to teach grammar effectively. This is a *how to* workshop that focuses on the instruction of specific grammatical structures and their immediate and continual usage by student-writers. It is grounded in the belief that clauses and phrases are tools writers employ in the work of writing, and that our job as instructors is to teach students about each tool, about its purpose, and then require that the tool be used as an integral part of the writing process.

Workshop 3
Prospero's Magic
**Critical Thinking Games
and Other Active Learning
Strategies for the Teaching
of Literature**

What is the English educator's purpose at the secondary level when teaching literature? If you believe it is to teach each student how to read sensitively, how to think creatively, and how to discuss what they read eloquently, this is your workshop. During this workshop the participants will play a number of critical thinking games based on literature, games that also reinforce speech and writing skills, skills required for statewide testing: clear thesis and topic sentences, coherence, detailed evidence, and originality. Directions and scoring of these and other activities will be provided.

FOR DETAILS CONCERNING EACH WORKSHOP AND HOW THEY CAN BE INDIVIDUALIZED TO MEET YOUR SCHOOL'S SPECIFIC NEEDS, CONTACT

Michael Degen, M.A.
gargery@yahoo.com
972-387-8700 ext 393

Printed in the United States
28062LVS00002B/277-288